THE PARADOXAL COMPASS

Drake's Dilemma

–

Horatio Morpurgo

nh Notting Hill Editions

Published in 2017
by Notting Hill Editions Ltd
Widworthy Barton Honiton Devon EX14 9JS

Designed by FLOK Design, Berlin, Germany
Typeset by CB editions, London

Printed and bound
by Memminger MedienCentrum, Memmingen, Germany

A CIP record for this book
is available from the British Library

ISBN 978-1-910749-51-7
www.nottinghilleditions.com

For Ioana, Hazel & Conrad

But keep in mind the waters where fish
See sceptres descending with no wish
To touch them; sit regal and erect,
But imagine the sands where a crown
Has the status of a broken-down
Sofa or mutilated statue:
Remember as bells and cannon boom
The cold deep that does not envy you . . .

– W. H. Auden

The sea speaks a language polite people never repeat.
It is a colossal scavenger slang and has no respect.

– Carl Sandberg

If you yourself can withstand three cheers at beholding
these vivacious fish, then heaven help ye; the spirit of godly
gamesomeness is not in ye.

– Herman Melville, on dolphins

Contents

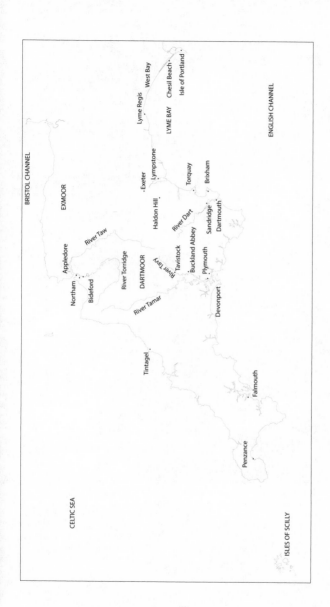

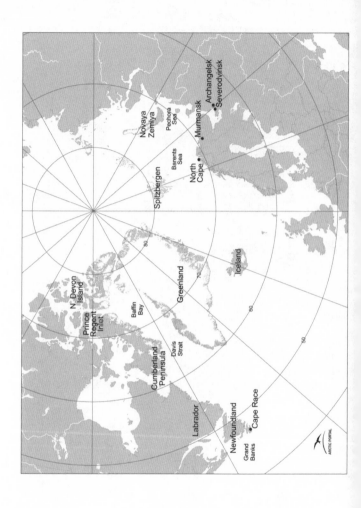

– Preface –

A family of eccentrics bought the folly in the 1930s and lived there for more than half a century. On a hill just outside Exeter, the tower and its crenellations overlooked half of Devon and Lyme Bay beyond but had never been intended for domestic use. Built as a memorial to the founder of the British Army in India, it was without running water or cooking facilities. Undeterred, its new owners carried water from a well, roasted squirrels on open fires and used the surrounding woodland as a latrine. They seem to have got by without a car. When restoration of the site finally began in the 1990s, an abandoned quarry, found a little way off in the woods, was completely overgrown with laurel and rhododendron and had evidently been used as a tip. It contained the frame of an old car, the remains of a summer house, several large lumps of granite and a statue in plaster.

This last was about 10 feet tall, pedestal included, and had been left standing upright in the bottom of the quarry. It was immediately recognised as the sculptor's model for the statue of Sir Francis Drake on Plymouth Hoe. Once the surrounding detritus had been cleared, it was found to be in reasonable condition. According to one source, it had arrived there before the Second

World War as a loan from the County Museum, which then never asked for it back. But inquiries were made and the museum had no record of ever having owned or loaned it.

This mysterious rediscovery was at first little publicised, but photographs from the time reveal an astonishing scene. Surrounded by foliage, the giant figure is ghostly pale, stained with algae, grown brittle here and there. Its bronze casting on the Hoe, a familiar landmark in Plymouth, had acquired a mysterious double. While the finished public statue had watched over great events, while it saw off the Blitz, while the Cold War came and went, its plaster original had become slowly lost in the understorey. The rhododendron and the laurel had crowded round every year a little closer. Forgotten in its hill-top hideaway, it became a kind of portrait in the national attic.

But who wanted it now? Where to store this fragile old negative, this perishable other, this chronically unfashionable image? The logistics alone were a headache nobody needed. Made in several sections, the legs to the waist were solid, so it was very heavy. The steel frame had to be specially designed, in which it could be winched onto the back of a lorry and taken away for restoration. It is now housed in Drake's old home at Buckland Abbey.

But its emergence from the undergrowth raised other questions than the logistic ones. Drake on the Hoe stands as the emblem of a certain unsinkable

England. There is the gold standard of national pride. Maybe we admire it, maybe we don't, but we leave it there. This great white idol pulled from its thicket on Haldon Hill, meanwhile, blemishes and all, is a different matter. He is unmistakably a companion piece to the other, but what are we to do with him?

This split in our response to the Age of Exploration is clearly visible in the way Drake is represented by TV historians. David Starkey, for his documentary about Queen Elizabeth, stands on the deck of a replica of the *Golden Hinde* and describes the circumnavigation as 'a pirate expedition to the Pacific . . . Drake's target was the Spanish treasure ships.' He explains what a very profitable business trip it was and it is plain, as we are told this, that we are to consider the matter closed. When another historian, Neil Hanson, tells us in a BBC interview that Drake made his fortune in the slave trade, and that this is what he was knighted for, his intentions are clearly the opposite of Starkey's. He is condemning. But there is, again, no hint of a doubt.

By and large, these two narratives, the champions and decriers, talk straight past each other. My case in this essay is that they do not need to. The purpose of Drake's circumnavigation remains contested and the evidence is far from conclusive either way. Drake did not make his fortune in and was not knighted for services to the slave trade. We can piece together something more truthful than either of these narratives and it is vital that we do so because 'history is precedent and permission', as Marilynne Robinson has memorably written about the 16th century. 'In this important instance,' she goes on, 'we have lost plain accuracy, not to speak of complexity, substance and human inflexion.'

—

Environmentalists routinely urge us, and with reason, to see our world a new way. We face a historic rupture, they say, unlike any that has gone before. I will argue here that at our own tipping-point we have much to learn from that turning-point four centuries ago. When the explorers first mapped the Arctic, when their instrument-makers supplied them with quadrants and compasses, this was courtesy of what they called natural philosophy and what we call science. The same inquiring outlook, partly derived from the ancients, partly a fresh invention, was turned also upon the creatures and plants being encountered for the first time by Europeans on those voyages. The stories they came home with would, in time, bring about a thoroughgoing reappraisal of our place in the world, and indeed the universe.

How did this feel at the time to those directly involved? The river valleys around Plymouth, with Dartmoor's outline to the north, together formed one of the first landscapes anywhere to absorb the gaze of people who had, literally, seen the world a new way. Those who returned with Drake from his Famous

Voyage knew, from lived experience, that even their longed-for home port was just one more point on the surface of a globe. We may never know whether they or those who welcomed them back appreciated the scale of this change, but there is evidence that somebody did.

Entering St Andrew's Plymouth you feel at once that the place is much restored. After it was left a burnt-out shell in 1942, it was turned into a garden at first, with flower beds in the nave and side aisles and roses trained up the pillars. But its full restoration was never in doubt. That it once emptied, in the middle of a sermon, at the news that Drake was home from the Americas, is part of the city's folklore. All his journeys done, Martin Frobisher's heart was buried there. But it was only as the post-war repairs got underway that a long-concealed, riddling message from the Age of Exploration could finally be read.

Carved into the stone sill of one of the south-facing windows, a diagram was found under the plasterwork. On a roughly drawn globe, the Equator and the two Tropics are energetically scored, criss-crossed with a couple of lines of longitude. From between the Equator and the Tropic of Cancer there emerge words in some jumbled and totally illegible script. Or is it some scratched out earlier version of the design? Below and to the right sits the figure of a ship, sail hoisted and topmast pennon streaming: from its prow extends a rope that swerves up and around the world, as if it has only just been thrown. A smaller boat floats free from the rest of the design, as if drawn to a different scale.

Known as 'the Drake Graffiti', its closeness to certain elements in the great sea captain's coat of arms was quickly remarked. Otherwise the half-century and more since its discovery has added little to our understanding of it. The travel guides all summarise it more or less thus: the local boy made good was home from sailing his ship around the world, the first sea captain ever to do so. In the ensuing Drake-mania this was a workman's doodle, done with the point of his trowel perhaps, before the plaster went on. This was an anonymous tribute to, or even consecration of, the staggering news that the *Golden Hinde* had made it back.

But for me at least there is also, in this rock-carving, in this 16th-century street art, a silent reproach to all the ways in which we still seek to tidy up this story. What was being celebrated as that figure was etched into medieval stonework? If this glyph is a witness statement from the original global moment, then what it suggests is that this was a much stranger event than we are accustomed to imagine. The very resistance of these markings to easy interpretation is precisely why we should cherish them. They remind us that we do not know. My case here is that this is a story we ignore because we think we know it. But we don't really know the story. There are other ways to tell it.

PART ONE

– Beginnings –

ALL APPARELLED IN WATCHET OR SKIE COLOURED CLOTH

Long before it became Stephen Borough's birth-place, Northam lived by its maritime connections. Its tall church tower was for centuries white-washed to serve as a landmark for ships entering the Torridge estuary. The village is surrounded on three sides by water, with the Bristol Channel to the west and the Taw and Torridge estuaries to the north and east.

Very little is known about Borough's early life. Certainly he was born in Northam in 1525 and grew up on a small farm just outside the village. A long stone building on the main square, now divided into flats, was once Church House and is probably where he learned to read and write. He would become one of the four 'principall masters' of Elizabeth's navy and was among Europe's best known navigators when he died in 1584.

The absence of any memorial to him in his first home is unsurprising in a way. His childhood surroundings lay far behind him by the time he made his first mark. That he had an uncle in shipping probably explains a good deal, though exactly how much we may never learn. We do know that, in May 1553, aged just twenty-eight, he was Master of one of three ships which sailed down the Thames past Greenwich. It was not an occasion he would ever have forgotten. An on-looker recorded the scene:

the Courtiers came out, and the common people flockt to-gether, standing very thicke upon the shoare: the privie Counsel [the King's closest advisors] they lookt out at the windowes of the Court, and the rest ranne up to the toppes of the towers.

On board, the mariners were 'all apparelled in Watchet or skie coloured cloth.' They 'shouted in such sort that the skie rang againe with the noyse thereof.' The expedition carried letters from Edward VI writ-ten in English, 'Greeke, and divers other languages', addressed to any 'Kings, Princes and Potentates' they might encounter on the way to China.

For this was the first English expedition to Asia. The chosen route was by the north-east and the ex-perts of the day confidently predicted that this route was wide open to anyone with the courage to risk it. From Norway's North Cape it was an easy run all the way to the Far East. These ships, accordingly, were 'prepared and furnished out, for the search and dis-coverie of the Northerne part of the world.' Their very names give a sense of the spirit in which this voyage was undertaken: the *Bona Esperanza*, the *Bona Confidentia* and the largest ship, of which Stephen was Master, the *Edward Bonaventura*.

The possibility of a northern route had already for some time been concentrating the best minds in the kingdom. The best minds were, all the same, wrong about it. What those buoyantly named vessels encountered on the way was nothing like what they had been led to expect. The ships became separated during a storm off Norway. For six weeks, two of them wandered disoriented in what we now call the Barents Sea. The crews eventually went ashore and built themselves a shelter for the winter. Russian fishermen found them the following spring, frozen to death. A journal found with them is in the British Library.

Stephen Borough's ship, staying closer to shore, rounded the North Cape and took shelter in a Danish settlement, the last one along this coast. They waited there for a week, 'troubled with cogitations and perturbations of mind', then steeled themselves to 'make proofe and triall of all adventures' and put to sea once more, holding their 'course for that unknowen part of the world.' Travelling along the coast they met with more Russian fishermen and overwintered just west of where the modern city of Archangel stands. The exact site, which they called St Nicholas, after a nearby convent, is now called Severovdinsk and is occupied by a gigantic facility which builds and re-fits submarines.

Perhaps the strangest thing about this voyage is that Russia appears to have come as a complete surprise. Invited to Moscow, the Englishmen were welcomed to the court of Ivan the Terrible, no less, and returned northwards with letters offering favourable terms for future trade. It was as much by chance as by design that England's first formally constituted foreign trading company, the Royal Muscovy Company, came to be.

The *Edward Bonaventura* returned safely home and his part in this 'first worthy enterprise' set Borough on course to become the company's senior pilot. In the 1560s he was spoken of as 'Cheyffe Pylott of this our Realm'. His memorial in Chatham credits him with the 'discouerie of Roosia and ye Coastes there to adjoininge'.

'Discovery' may seem to put it rather strongly, when there were so many friendly fishermen on hand to help the explorers as and when they got into trouble. This was hardly an un-peopled wilderness awaiting its colonial master. Before we smile too broadly at this use of the word, however, we should remind ourselves that these English strangers and their arrival from the north did indeed portend change.

Tsar Ivan knew strong magic when he saw it. Russia at the time was in conflict with Sweden, Poland-Lithuania and the Holy Roman Empire. It could definitely use a technically competent ally to the west of its immediate neighbours. The rumour has persisted that Ivan made a marriage offer to Elizabeth, which was rejected. He abruptly suspended the Muscovy

Company's rights in his empire. They were quietly restored once the imperial tantrum had passed and business as usual resumed. Ivan's son Feodor also sought stronger ties. The chief advisor to England's navigators, John Dee, an instructor to Borough as to many others, was offered a handsome fee to go and work in Moscow. He too would decline the invitation.

On his second voyage, in 1556–7, Borough's ship carried a kind of research vessel, around 40 feet long and with a draft of no more than 5 feet. It was in this, the *Searchthrift*, that Stephen Borough sailed on from Wardhouse in Norway with a crew of just ten. In not much more than a fly-boat, then, they proceeded carefully eastwards, realising that only by keeping close to the shore could they avoid the disaster which had befallen the first expedition.

The popular account of this period still associates small English ships with the defeat of the Armada. In fact, thirty years earlier, English explorers had already learnt the hard way that larger ships can put you at a disadvantage. Smaller, lighter vessels allowed you to manoeuvre round floating ice or to go closer inshore, though the shallow draft also made them vulnerable to storms. The technical means available to these earliest explorers were extremely modest: they 'made for that unknowen part of the world', seeking guidance and asking permission as they went, with astonishingly delicate instruments.

Other kinds of danger than storms might also

arise. Borough's logbook described the following close encounter:

On S. James his day [22nd July] . . . at a Southwest sunne, there was a monstrous Whale aboord of us, so neere to our side that we might have thrust a sworde or any other weapon in him, which we durst not doe for feare hee should have over-thrown our shippe: and then I called my company together, and all of us shouted, & with the crie that we made he parted from us: there was as much above water of his backe as the bredth of our pinnesse, and at his falling downe, he made such a terrible noyse in the water, that a man would greatly have marvelled, except hee had knowen the cause of it: but God be thanked, we were quietly delivered of him.

This would probably have been a Northern Right or Bowhead whale, plentiful then in the high latitudes. And it was an ominous encounter, freighted with implications for both parties. This fearsome creature is plainly still as much the biblical Leviathan as it is any kind of actual whale. 'Canst thou draw out leviathan with a hook?' asks the Book of Job. 'Shall the companions make a banquet of him? shall they part him among the merchants?'

For a little while, the answer to that in these waters at least was still no.

———

It is not easy to visit Stephen Borough's childhood home because a Captain Yeo demolished it and built his mansion directly on top of it in the 1860s. But you can still walk part of the footpath Borough took from that vanished farmstead down to the ships at Appledore. The street you'll need is right at the edge of Northam, lined with bungalows and signed as a dead-end. But where the bungalows and the tarmac stop, a farm track and then the footpath take you down to the estuary.

In late May, a gap in the hedge opens onto a blaze of buttercups and the atmosphere is heady with quick-thorn in flower. A blackcap is singing and the hogweed is waist-deep. The path ends where the River Torridge, full from its long loop south and then north through mid-Devon, empties into the shipping lanes and fishing grounds of the Bristol Channel. To anyone who knows about Borough, this looks like a landscape designed with the production of navigators in mind.

But very few people here do know about him. The first biography appeared only ten years ago, written by a medical professional retired to the area after a life of university teaching. He lives on the road which leads to that footpath, walking his dog up and down it most days. One of the things I want to ask, when I go to meet him, is why does he think the village makes so little of this story?

He has already asked more questions than most interviewees ever do. He's well-travelled himself, the room is book-lined and he's curious about what I'm doing. But he pauses now, weighing his words. 'If we were in Russia or China,' he says, 'I suppose the local children would all be taught to recite a list of his achievements . . .'

I think I know where he's going: 'And there'd be a hideous statue of him in the main square,' I put in.

'Exactly,' he agrees, laughing. 'As it is, it's mostly incomers, people like me, who take an interest.'

He seems to be saying he prefers it this way and I share his doubts about hero-worship. I prefer it like this, too. Stephen Borough lingers as a scarcely detectable trace round the edges of what is now a bedroom suburb and part of me likes him all the more for it. He and his like do their spiriting so gently most people are unaware they're doing it at all.

———

The absence of any memorial to Borough in Northam might appeal to reticent types who enjoy their country walks. But really *nothing*? Where would be the harm in some discreet signposting for those who might like to know more? Even his erasure from the scene – and from the popular story of 16th-century discovery more generally – is itself a story worth telling. His absence here goes back a long way and is directly traceable to a statue that *was* put up, and which overlooks the Torridge to this day, just a mile or two upstream.

Charles Kingsley, an Anglican patriarch in marble vestments, still muses upon his plinth on the water front at Bideford. He stands at the entrance to a car park these days, just part of the urban scene, but Kingsley was an un-ignorable public figure once. The nearby holiday resort of Westward Ho! gets its strange name from the title of his 1855 novel. When Captain Yeo built a mansion on the site of Borough's birthplace five years later, Kingsley's story, set in the Age of Discovery, would have had everything to do with it.

Half of the first chapter takes place in Northam, in what is obviously Borough's home, and the story repeatedly returns to it. Yet the novel's six-hundred-odd pages include not one solitary mention of Borough himself. Kingsley grew up in Devon and was a Professor of History at Cambridge. He would have known everything there was to know about Borough. His novel is full of maritime heroes brought to life: his recreations of Grenville, Drake and Oxenham, for example, are successful. He was well able to do it when he wished to.

So why didn't he wish to in this case? Borough Farm is bumped up to 'Burrough Court' and becomes in the novel the childhood home of one Amyas Leigh, the tale's hero. Leigh is a kind of Hooray Henry: landed gentry, a downright countryman, a Spain-hater through and through, 'grossly ignorant' of science and religion. After knocking his schoolteacher uncon-scious, he is spirited away via aristocratic contacts and takes ship with Drake, sailing around the world as a gentleman adventurer, thereby acquiring the reflex anti-Catholicism of the age.

Kingsley would have known that the Boroughs were above all super-competent artisans. They were not swaggering sea-dog material. The family contact that counted for Stephen was an experienced Bristol-based shipmaster, which is to say a technician. As we'll see, Borough was very far from ignorant of science or religion and he would have been no Spain-hater either. His first expedition carried letters from Edward VI, but the Protestant boy king was too weak to join in the send-off at Greenwich. He was already ill and would be dead in a matter of weeks. The England to which the *Edward Bonaventura* returned was Catholic once more, ruled over now by Queen Mary and her husband, Philip of Spain. Indeed, one of the ships in the follow-up expedition, two years later, was even called the *Philip and Mary.*

Upon his return from this second voyage, Borough was invited to the *Casa de Contratación* in Seville, the headquarters of Spanish maritime enterprise. He brought back a copy of Martin Cortes' *Compendio della Sphera e del Arte de Navigar.* This was translated by a friend of his as *The Art of Navigation* and remained the standard scientific manual for navigators for the rest of the century. Spain-hater? Despiser of book learning?

Kingsley needed a vehicle for his own (vehement) anti-Catholicism and his very mid-Victorian brand of muscular Christianity. So he elevated his boy from Northam into the landed gentry and then supplied him with views and behavioural issues which the young

Stephen would have found very puzzling indeed. This substitution, together with the mansion which still occupies the site of his birthplace, effectively removed Stephen Borough from popular consciousness. He was disappeared by an act of posthumous gentrification.

There is, in other words, more than meets the eye in the curious absence of Stephen Borough from his own birthplace. The real Borough would have been conversant with, and riven by, the many conflicts through which his society was passing. He and his kind were long ago switched with the Sir Amyas Leighs in the story we have told about modern England's founding moment. Nothing obliges us to keep passing this on. There is indeed no reason to drill schoolchildren or raise hideous statues, but it might well be time to see what has been left out of this story. Other surprises await us in Devon's less trendy corners.

For what is true of this village is true of the region as a whole. It presents visitors and residents alike with a contradiction. It is both a rural heartland and the point of many famous departures. The south west peninsula was the first English province to globalise but it remains in the popular imagination closely associated with the contrary, too, with English life at its most settled. Shot through with this paradox, the West Country inspires great loyalty. Its landscape retains unusual magnetic properties, especially for people who grew up there.

A NEW START OUT WEST

We went to live in Devon in the mid-Seventies. Suddenly my bedroom overlooked changes in the atmosphere pulling Dartmoor in and out of focus. I attended the local school and played football with new friends. I went on swapping one hobby for the next, much as I had in our previous home. Stamps for a bit, then coins: I collected all kinds of junk. In an old atlas, for example, a certain ragged archipelago was still busy spraying the world pink with its shipping lanes. My personal favourite among our many possessions was a 'North Devon Island' in the Canadian Arctic. This was, apparently, the largest uninhabited island in the world.

Mains electricity had arrived in the village less than ten years earlier, so that older, more self-reliant way of living which we had come in search of was still a recent memory. My mother bought an old paraffin lamp and a new roll of thick cotton wick, polished up the metal parts and got it working again. When the outside world did occasionally reach us, in the form of power cuts, it found us prepared. The soft, adjustable light on uneven cob walls was a sign of our resistance.

If the view by day was Dartmoor, at night it was a scatter of farmyard lights in the rural blackout. I forget what age I was when I first ran a pair of binoculars through the stars above our back gate. That place was as close as you could still get to pre-Edison England.

Nostalgic? Escapist? With hindsight, maybe, but hindsight can be overrated. I loved it.

You might ask, as I later did, of course, whether severing oneself and one's off-spring from the present in this way, or trying to, isn't a rather extreme programme. But consider the context: these were the days of oil shock and looming nuclear catastrophe. The Vietnam War had only just ended. I forget now whether I understood at the time what all those power cuts were about. Or what I thought at first of the military jets on their exercises.

Then why not take to the hills? And why not take to self-reliance and paraffin lamps while you're about it? The move came also, for my parents, after a series of unsatisfactory teaching jobs. Here they could put into practise the kind of open-air classroom in which they actually believed. They went into partnership with a local farming family to organise visits for inner city children.

To say we were 'severed from the present' implies, firstly, that such a thing is possible, but also that time only passes in one way and we all know which that way is. But do we? There were so many different forms of time here. The time of history continued, on news programmes we saw fewer of these days, but we knew it was there. Cattle went under cover for the winter or in summer were let out into the fields, where I learnt not to be afraid of them as I wandered further and further from home.

There was the time, too, in which my father's books were conceived and written and the time it takes to swap one hobby for another. There was the time it takes for fashions in music to change, too – a kind of time from which my brother, in particular, refused point blank to be separated. So many different kinds of time to disagree with each other, then make it up, then disagree again. For there was family time, here, too.

At night, even in that first summer, in the worst drought for decades, you could always hear water. A sprightlier Torridge than the one which ebbs and flows at Northam ran past the end of our lane and somewhere at the back of everything here was the river-sound. Louder than the nearest road, that background murmur worked tirelessly, connecting up our lives to what always had been here and always would be.

—

I discovered *Proud Heritage* shortly after we arrived, in a stone shed attached to the end of the cottage. A fragile anthology of national heroes, left behind by the previous occupants, it was held together with badly rusted spiral binding. It was, even when I found it, in an advanced state of decay. But here was my personal gift from the new home. The back pages had crumbled away with the damp, possibly helped along by mice. Charles Dickens was the last of the fully legible heroes and even he was breaking up.

It had been printed for the coronation of George

VI. Wycliffe, Chaucer and Shakespeare qualified for rather stilted portraits, each opposite his bio note. Milton and Newton and Wilberforce. Michael Faraday and John Constable and Charles Darwin: staring past you, features aglow, transfigured by their part in the glorious story.

I added my name in a bold scrawl to the two already present on the title page and applied various bandages. Then I read the book again, right here, in the same house where it had been read before by my predecessors and against the same background of river-sound.

The bandages I applied then are by now sorely in need of bandaging themselves. To my present taste, an air of post-Victorian taxidermy hovers about those portraits, an odour of congealed moral grandeur. But I'm still glad I salvaged them. It's little more than a bound collection of out-size cigarette cards. Thirties ephemera. The heritage to be proud of in those days was boysey, so to speak, and somewhat 'monochrome'.

Say, though, just for the sake of argument, that we forgive 1937 for not being 2017. Say we look at this coronation souvenir as reflecting how a certain culture saw itself. We don't, for the purposes of this exercise, even have to think of it as our own.

Very few people, then as now, would claim to know much about Henry II or George Fox or Elizabeth Fry, let alone all three. You can hardly read it at all now without damaging it, but such a booklet expressed an aspiration. I do still occasionally pick through its pages and as I do so, even as it sheds a few more papery crumbs, I'm still struck by how much I do not know. The personages collected there would have disagreed pretty severely about a lot. Together, though, they suggest the possibility of a conversation to which this booklet was a kind of welcome.

When someone evokes a more harmonious past, a more rural one perhaps, when we shared assumptions, we are surely entitled to ask who 'we' are and which past that was? Was this the Reformation, perhaps? What was it precisely that the martyrs and their executioners agreed on? Was it the Civil War, rather? Or the decades of struggle for religious tolerance which followed? Was it the small matter of enclosure about which 'we' all saw eye to eye? Or the campaign to end slavery? Or the other one, to abolish child labour? When was it that we all agreed about so much? When exactly did we English jog so merrily together along the leafy tow-path of history?

But if *Proud Heritage* is any guide to how the English saw themselves in 1937, I'd say they were better prepared than they knew for what was about to happen. True, there are very few women and no blacks or browns. No reference to Lollards or Levellers or Chartists and I know, now, that this is not an accident. But the aspiration to know more has to begin somewhere and it has to begin with the realisation that you actually know very little. This isn't a flattering message at any age. What we long to hear is, on the contrary, that we know quite enough by now, thank you very much. That we've heard everything we need to hear and understand 'only too well.'

But I still think that unwelcome, slightly daunted feeling is the one to trust. It is the price of admission. Because in the long run, being better informed, or even just wishing you were, tends to build immunity against kitsch. This is what the crumbling pages of that booklet say to me now. Ours is a world capable of producing a Henry VIII or a John Bunyan. The moment you start wondering how, you automatically enrol in a kind of immunisation programme against cultural and political kitsch. It doesn't matter where you start. So long as you do start.

THE ACCIDENTAL DISCOVERY OF THE SCILLY ISLES

During squally weather in June 1585, two small vessels put in at the Isles of Scilly. Most of the crew stayed on board and the men who went ashore for fresh water said little, only that they had already been penned in Falmouth for five days by the same strong wind which had now forced them to take shelter here. The wind was blowing out of the north-west, so it followed that their business lay that way. The next day dawned clear, with warmer air from the south. The ships were gone again at first light.

Both they and the foul weather returned the following day, however, the wind having once more swung round contrary. When the vessels docked at New Grimsby this time, the main harbour on Tresco, the islanders' curiosity was still further piqued. They would have had keen eyes for such 'low profile' comings and goings. They did not look like fishing boats and it was too late in the season for those anyway. The larger of the ships was of fifty tonnes perhaps, the smaller of about thirty. It was difficult to find out more. The crew was kept very busy.

Cornwall generally, and especially Falmouth, was a well-known pirate base. And to anyone who knows the Scilly Isles, New Grimsby was, even then, an unusual choice of mooring. Tresco was described only a few years earlier as 'a bushment of briars and a refuge for all the pirates that ranged.' It was bandit country. The difficulty of defending livestock and other possessions against marauders had dramatically thinned out the island's population.

But the position of this archipelago, at the entrance to the Channel, also made it strategically indispensable. A Spanish plan to occupy and use it as a naval base and advance post had come to nothing only ten years earlier. Any country wishing to control sea traffic in the Western Approaches had to control the Scillies. It could be assumed that Spain still had the islands under close watch.

It was true the ships had been detained in

Falmouth but they had in fact sailed from Dartmouth, John Davis' home port. He was captain of the larger of the two vessels, the *Sunneshine*, and the leader of the expedition. And he had a plan.

Davis had that rare quality among great explorers: he seems to have been likeable. This might explain why the last biography appeared a hundred and something years ago. He was probably born in a farmhouse at Sandridge just upstream from Dartmouth, now a high-end holiday-let, on which there is no plaque. Of the original unpretentious dwelling only the basement (possibly) survives. Little is known of his career up to this point: no Oxford or Cambridge for him. As with Borough, all we know of his education is what we can infer from his having grown up close to a busy port. What we do know is that in 1585 he was in his mid-thirties, had been at sea for twenty years already and that his interest in the new science was proven. He would write books about it one day. But though he became one of the foremost navigators of his age, he was never a rich man. Sir Francis Drake definitely earned himself a page in *Proud Heritage.* John Davis Esq. did not.

Those two ships which put in at New Grimsby, the *Sunneshine of London* and the *Mooneshine of Dartmouth*, made up his first command. The expedition had not got off to a flying start but his solution was in character. From onshore, their behaviour must have seemed perplexing indeed. Every morning, the ship's boat was launched, rough weather notwithstanding. It set its course each day for a different corner of the island-group. It was seen to remain stationary for long periods as soundings were taken and observations of the coastline made.

Davis took this opportunity, in other words, to draw up the first detailed chart of the Scilly Isles ever made. In Elizabethan English, if you 'discover' something to someone else, you reveal or show it to them, you make that visible which was formerly concealed. The islands had never, until June 1585, merited anything more than a guesswork of island-shapes, loosely assembled thirty-odd miles west of Land's End. No doubt Davis undertook this task partly to guard against his crew's boredom, to prevent any doubts from taking root during this early set-back. Keeping the men occupied would also reduce the risk of any loose talk with locals.

This unscheduled stop-over made, then, for an ideal opportunity to impress upon the minds of his crew the purpose of their voyage and what would be expected of them. Its purpose was to 'discover', i.e. find and then map, a passage to India and China through the 'Straits of Annian', the legendary North West Passage. Early cartographers had assumed this must extend around the top of what is now Canada. Once discovered – and its existence was an article of quasi-mystical faith at this time – the strait would open up a trade route to the Far East which would cut out the Spanish. Hence the need for secrecy.

For such a technical rehearsal these islands, in blustery weather and choppy seas, with all those tricky shallows and numberless rocks, were ideal. And their selection was not as random as it might look. The islanders themselves would have been well aware that their home was the natural testing-ground for the latest defence-related technologies.

This last English outcrop before the Atlantic was contested territory. Three years later the Armada would sail with orders to *rendez-vous* off the Scillies, but was blown off course before most of its ships could reach them. Their uncertain status is surely there also in the way the islands were spelt. In addition to the way we spell them now they were at this date either given their French name, Sorlinges, or had to put up whatever Elizabethan spelling felt like that day: Scylla, Cillie, Sillie, and, yes, even plain Silly. They do not appear at all, under any name, on Saxton's great atlas of England and Wales, published in 1579.

Davis of all people, at this of all times, would have been aware of that omission and of the need to include the islands now. In June 1585 the whole country was in the grip of one of those xenophobic convulsions which we now call security alerts. The Spanish siege of Antwerp continued. The Catholic party in France was in the ascendant. And now English merchant ships had been seized and impounded by Spanish port authorities. Some response there must be. One day after Davis had left Dartmouth, Francis Drake sailed up the Thames to organise and take command of a punitive expedition involving more than thirty ships. That autumn he would embark upon one of his most disgraceful orgies of destructive violence.

That same June, Richard Grenville was leading a fleet up the coast of Virginia in search of a location for the first English settlement in North America. Indeed, the name 'Virginia' had been dreamed up only a few months earlier. Grenville burnt down an Indian village as he went, in reprisal for the theft of a silver cup. Spanish spies had anxiously reported his departure from Plymouth in April, unable to determine his journey's purpose. Another fleet had been sent to raid Spanish shipping around Newfoundland in the same month. They returned with hundreds of prisoners and several thousand tonnes of dried fish.

For all of its modest scale and technical sophistication, Davis' expedition, too, was part of this national project to 'annoy' the world's only superpower. His accidental 'discovery' of the Scilly Isles might appear harmless enough, and indeed, by comparison it was. But even such early forays into the new science are shadowed by their consequences. A week after leaving Tresco, 'a very great Whale' was recorded, 'and every day we saw whales continually.' Ten days later they were still seeing 'great store of Whales.' Four centuries later, the use of that term 'store' comes with its own twinge of presentiment.

For there exists a perspective now, a background

awareness of everything that followed, against which the 'Age of Discovery' appears much diminished, even fundamentally questionable. A new impermanence, seeping into our lives through everything we thought we knew, reaches out not only around the world but back across the centuries. It is impossible to miss the multiple ironies in those explorer accounts.

—

Davis and his men heard the other side of the Atlantic before they saw it. Three weeks after leaving Scilly, the ships 'fell into a great whirling and brustling of a tyde' before they entered 'a very calme Sea', in which they could hear, nevertheless, 'a mighty great roaring.'

This, they assumed, must be waves breaking on a shore but the air was 'so foggie and full of thicke mist' that the two ships could not even see each other let alone what was further ahead. The ship's boat was now lowered again and soundings taken, but the lead which had found ten fathoms off New Grimsby 'could not find ground in 300 fathoms' here.

The two ships proceeded carefully, each firing a musket into the fog every thirty minutes, to let the other know where it was. Weird forms began to loom: they 'met many Ilands of yce floting', midsummer pack-ice streaming south from Greenland. Davis sent men to explore these 'islands', which was when they realised that 'all the roaring which we heard, was caused onely by the rowling of this yce together.' They returned to the ships 'laden with ice, which made very good fresh water', the first they had taken on board since Tresco. It was only next day that the fog lifted, allowing them to see land.

From a granite archipelago, they passed over to another, of ice. So the stories we have lived by acquire a new fragility. In the following year, West Country merchants funded yet another search for the North West Passage. In a location which had been open sea a year before, Davis encountered 'a most mighty and strange quantity of yce, so bigge that we knew not the limits thereof.' He took it to be a new country, even sending his boat to 'discover' it. This vast and mysterious object, in other words, came within a whisker of being mapped and claimed for Her Majesty. The boat's crew soon returned. It was 'onely yce', they reported. But the news 'bred great admiration to us all.' It took them nearly two weeks to sail around it. The quantity of ice, Davis wrote, was 'incredible to be reported . . . and therefore I omit to speake any further thereof'. To see the New World, as others before him had already found, was at the same time to reach the limits of language.

Ancient geographers were little help in these newly discovered regions. It is difficult for us, who perhaps glance past images of the Arctic most days, to grasp now how perplexing that scenery encountered for the first time must have been. Davis gives some hints of this in that phrase 'incredible to be reported'. One ancient explorer, a Greek called Pytheas, did claim to have travelled so far north that there was no land or sea or air but a substance which comprised all of these, 'holding them in suspension.' Pytheas called this substance 'sea-lungs'. Stay-at-home scholars, listening to the explorers, assumed that their 'Mowntaynes of Ise, somme of a myle long; somme longer', must be what the Greeks had meant by 'sea-lungs'.

But we are, also, in our way, at a point now where none of the categories that have served in the past help us to describe what we now see. Hence our collective difficulty in seeing it at all. Greenland welcoming the *Sunneshine of London* and the *Mooneshine of Dartmouth* with the growl of its pack-ice is loaded, for us, with ominous meaning which will have eluded Davis entirely. An ice-berg that takes two weeks to sail around, which can be mistaken for a country, can only have been part of an ice-shelf.

We too are without words adequate for what this 'quantity of yce' portends. We know, as Davis could not, that the Scillies, as he mapped them and as they still appear today, are a drowned landscape, the hill-tops of a much larger island, submerged as sea-levels rose during the later Middle Ages. Tresco, from which he set sail, had been, a century or two earlier, part of a 'St Nicholas' Island', joined by a land bridge with what is now the neighbouring island of Bryher.

A copy of John Davis' map has survived. You can still see how the weather that June confined his ship's boat to the more sheltered waters. The mapping of areas exposed to the west is much thinner in detail. The Western Rocks, for example, stretching from Bryher all the way to the horizon – a notorious maritime graveyard – appear as pebbles tidied into absurd little heaps. The depth at their farthest limit is marked as 18 fathoms, as if to show that they did, in spite of everything, make it that far.

The map may suggest something else, too, about those twelve days. The only features to be marked with place names in both English and Cornish are the islands of Tresco and Bryher. Indeed the Cornish versions appear above the English ones and are in bold: **Trystraw** and **Bryadk**. They cannot have spent the better part of two weeks there without speaking to *anyone*. Is this concession to local sensibilities all the trace that remains of their communication?

These days any day-tripper to Hugh Town can grab a better map than this off the counter at Tourist Information. It does not, by our standards, correspond very closely to what is actually there. Some of the islands seem a bit squashed and those cartoon Western Rocks are no danger to anybody.

But it is no wonder that Davis kept quiet about what he was up to here. He was, after all, seeing this farthest corner of England as it had never been 'seen' before. This was a fateful moment. He took this corner of his home country and treated it as a set of points, to be triangulated like any other such set, anywhere in the world. If there was a new exactitude here, there was a new detachment, too.

A DRAKEAN ACT HAS CONSEQUENCES

The sharp drop in temperature as the new school term approached was excellent news. The blizzard they were forecasting would soon block every possible exit. And so it did. For several days I stayed on at home, enjoying an indefinitely extended Christmas holiday. I photographed the astonishing forms of the snow-drifts which had filled our lane. Even from the pages of an old album they still seem to glow with something of the gratitude I felt towards them. School was on the far side of the moor and the moor for now was impassable.

But a friend of my parents worked for the Forestry Commission and had access to a Land Rover. One greeny-grey morning, I was finally persuaded to climb into its freezing cab and watch my knees turn white as we rattled manfully along the treacherous roads. Changing schools as often as I did at that age – this was my third new one in four years – functioned like a kind of school in itself. Not a bad one, I might add. At an early age I got to meet lots of interesting people, albeit never for very long.

Several of the teachers at this latest place, for example, had come 'home' from Kenya after independence. One of them, formerly a farmer in the Rift Valley, taught us English literature and the Old Testament. The Rift Valley was home to the original humans, he heretically informed us, the true Garden of Eden. Its climate was the one we evolved in, which is why it still feels so perfect. He brought in books all about it to show us.

The New Testament was taught by HPW, another exile from the same East African Garden. He had no gift for classroom teaching and a rotten temper with it. But he did have a bird-table outside the window of his office and instead of telling us about the New Testament, invited us in one afternoon to watch it with him. The next week he took an interested group of boys bird-watching in the school grounds. Then he took groups of us out on a little boat he kept moored on the Tavy.

It was old-fashioned in other ways, too. It was quickly clear my parents had opted for a bracing conservatism this time around. Plymouth was close by and the dormitories were all named after naval heroes. Borough and Davis were not among them. The shoulder patches on our Navy-blue jerseys were intentionally martial-looking and the prefects wore little badges with anchors on them. The school took its maritime connections seriously. Our sports teams were feared.

Such an atmosphere was not so very strange for Devon in the late Seventies. There was a Cold War on as well as a run of bad winters. NATO and the Warsaw Pact played war games in the North Atlantic, Devonport prospered mightily and we dressed the part.

Most of the boys were being paid for by the Ministry of Defence. Somebody's father came to teach us about the Russian Navy, how to tell a Victor Class submarine from an Alpha Class one. Another father landed his green helicopter on a games field one afternoon.

Drake's Prayer was read at Remembrance Day services and books about him were handed out as school prizes. I still have mine. Most of us were from nearby and it was expected, I suppose, that we identify with the Age of Discovery, with the disproportionate role played in it by ships based in the Western Ports.

To one suggestible eleven-year-old the offer of being inscribed in such a pedigree was attractive. HPW's boat was moored just above Plymouth. He had, it was rumoured, 'requisitioned' it in northern Germany at the end of the war and sailed it home. I'm afraid I approved of this Drakean act, though it is, sadly, now too late to ask whether it actually happened. Wherever he got it from, we helped him re-launch it in the spring, just a few miles from the abbey Drake bought with the proceeds of his Famous Voyage.

We explored the thickly wooded labyrinth of waterways and tidal creeks that reach into the countryside behind Plymouth. To geographers this is a 'drowned valley system', submerged at the end of the last ice age. When I later came across that 'nook-shotten isle' phrase in Shakespeare it was immediately those outings I thought of. Some experiences turn into memory by an incremental process – sedimentary or metamorphic rather than igneous memories. Those long afternoons, tidal waters obeying their own slow laws around us, were my earliest intimation of this.

But on one trip we sailed right down into Plymouth Sound, past the rusting steel cliffs of a decommissioned aircraft carrier, past the nuclear submarine pens and finally past 'Drake's Island', encrusted with mouldering air defence batteries. This, our teacher explained, was where the greatest explorer of them all had paused as he sailed into his home port at the end of the circumnavigation, with no idea what he was coming 'home' to.

With hindsight, there was more than a touch of the displaced person about HPW. I wonder what he really made of the country he'd come 'home' to. Perhaps that's how he successfully instilled so much affection for particular places. He would take a group to the Scillies in the spring holidays and we always seemed to get lucky with the weather. It was on one of those trips that I first saw Bryher for myself. You can easily walk round it in a day. The weather was so good that even the character-building spam with which he insisted on filling our sandwiches seemed almost edible. A young merlin, my first, skimmed the heather or wheeled overhead as we made our circuit, winding up the charm.

Bryher is, to the west, open to everything the elements have to throw at it. There are bare rocks and un-inhabited islands all the way to the horizon. The other way faces on to white sandy lagoons and the sheltered moorings of Tresco Channel. I still have a photograph I took that first day, of the daffodils out on my enchanted island. There is New Grimsby behind them, just across the water.

This place was everything I already loved about the Scillies from earlier trips, but in concentrated form. You admire quite indiscriminately at that age. You think the sheltered moorings and those jagged rocks out there are, somehow or other, going to complement each other. It will all add up one day. Such confidence doesn't last and perhaps that's just as well. Drake embarking with a fleet that will torch three cities, Grenville burning down an Indian village, Davis patiently 'discovering' the Isles of Scilly – at twelve you just 'love history', or you 'love the Tudors', or you 'love Bryher', or something like that. You've no idea what you're getting into.

Sunshine or Moonshine? Drake or Davis? Paradisal lagoon one way, shipping hazard the other. Bryher was a good place to start learning how to hold both sides of a question before the mind's eye. Connected to the world by ocean currents and the migratory routes of birds, it still retains, for me, something of that twelve-year-old's anticipation of life. I couldn't wait to tell my parents all about it.

—

Drake once sailed from Florida to the Scillies in just twenty-three days, heading home from a raid on the 'silver train'. This was the route by which the Spanish transported bullion, on mules, from Panama City across the isthmus to Nombre de Dios. From there it was loaded on to ships for transport across the Atlantic. It was during this raid in 1573 that Drake caught his first glimpse of the Pacific. The sighting, by all accounts, struck him with a revelatory power. He was coming home now, at speed, but he knew what he had to do next.

He had with him, on that return journey, Diego, a Cimaroon. The Cimaroons were escaped slaves who had established their own settlements in remote forests. Nobody knew the terrain better and Drake formed an alliance with them which alarmed the Spanish colonial authorities. Diego sued to be taken on board in 1573 and would sail with Drake on later expeditions, on the same terms and for the same pay as English crew. The Scillies would have been his first sight of England. With the outline of their low hills, with the white sand and glittering waters between them, he must have thought his new home was going to be a bit like the Caribbean.

—

At the end of my last term there, the leavers were all taken on an outing to Drake's home at Buckland Abbey. My diary tells me he casually walked into the Great Hall as I lingered to admire the portraits: 'I had an amazing feeling . . . Francis Drake walked in. I could imagine everything.' It's a pretty bare mention, considering. You'd think I might have recorded some part of what he said at least. Did I not have any questions? I remembered the atmosphere and the portraits in that hall but I'd clean forgotten, until I was looking through that diary years later, that he put in a personal appearance.

His reputation has risen, has fallen, has shape-shifted down the centuries and continues to do so. But that habits of veneration can be transmitted in this way, such that a schoolboy four hundred years later was still picking up residual traces of the cult, is surely passing strange.

Or possibly not. We were more haunted by that ghost ship then than we are today. Only a decade earlier, the *Golden Hinde* was as common as the half-pennies on which it still figured. Not only was its silhouette Devon's county emblem but a silver model of the ship, revolving on a turntable to the sound of trumpets, preceded any programme made by local independent TV. This channel even made an interesting film about the circumnavigation, called 'Drake's Venture', just before losing its franchise in 1980.

But my strongest memory of this presence is nothing to do with public culture. On our way back from one of those trips to the Scillies, the ferry was caught in a Force Nine gale. Entertaining a stoical self-image at the time, I stayed up on deck and storm-watched all the way back to Penzance. A crossing which normally takes two and a half hours took eight but I wedged myself as tight as I could into a corner, which shielded me from the worst of it. Big as our ship and bigger, waves towered and teetered or shattered on impact and went hissing and slithering across our decks. The RMV *Scillonian* needs a relatively shallow draft for the waters around the islands, but its design can make rough crossings very rough indeed.

It was quite like the vessels used by explorers, in other words: through half-closed eyes I could just about imagine this the Yeere of Our Lorde Fifteen Hundred and Seventie Eight and our Galleon battling an hurricano thru the Streights of Magellane. It helped to pass the time. We seemed not so much to be advancing towards our destination as foiling violent and repeated attempts to make the boat go backwards. From the security of my improvised look-out I watched the line of the deck rear right up then drop alarmingly, well below the horizon.

The whole boat shuddered as each wave hit but then came the reassuring tremor of engines still working. At the foot of a cliff, as the coastline crawled by, lay the up-turned hull of the *Union Star*: I'd gone carol-singing a few months earlier for the families of its crew and the families of those who died on the lifeboat that went to its rescue. I'd fallen into a kind of trance, I suppose, staring into each wall of water as it approached, the ship rolling and recoiling from the last or lurching into the next. And here came one now that looked much like the others, until a dolphin leapt out of it. I stared in disbelief, waiting for confirmation, but it was one dolphin for one leap only, then gone again, back into that seething mass of verticals and horizontals, planes randomly colliding and buckling as they did so. But somewhere inside it all now was a dolphin and I had a story to explain why I'd stuck to this strange vigil.

OUR ENCOMPASSING OF THIS NEATHER GLOBE

Folktales about Drake flourished in the West Country even during his own life-time. He was widely thought of as an enchanter. Once he did make it into the Pacific, and then got home, his having 'shot the gulf' was proof of occult powers. He was thought to possess a mirror which allowed him to see over the horizon and Spanish prisoners were told by their English guards that he was a sorcerer. In calling him 'The Dragon', his enemies didn't just mean he was a pyromaniac and all-round baddie. They meant he was an emblem of Diabolus.

Devil's Point, overlooking Plymouth Sound, is a promontory from which the families of Navy personnel still wave off their loved ones. It was said that Drake went there at the approach of the Spanish Armada and cut pieces of wood into the water. By the power of magic these became at once the well-armed gun boats by which he saw off the invader. As Mayor of the city he would later bring clean water off the moor by constructing a leat. Even such municipal good works morphed into stories about how the water had followed magically at his horse's heels as he rode into town one morning.

Such stories were only one outlet among many for the widespread unease to which the new mathematical sciences gave rise – navigation and engineering included. But it was not only a function of that. There are non-western cultures in which long-distance travel is also an activity with magical associations – not least in that very Pacific region through which Drake sailed. The Trobriand Islands, Hawaii and Eastern Papua New Guinea have all furnished anthropologists with examples.

His uncanny aura can only have been strengthened by the secrecy surrounding his Famous Voyage. The logbook, illustrated by himself and his cousin John and presented to the Queen at Whitehall during six hours of conversation, has, famously, vanished. The world map which he gave her at the same time was still hanging there fifty years later but has also since disappeared.

The resulting gaps in our knowledge have generated a compensatory hunger for information about exactly what happened. A readiness, too, to speculate about how such documents come to be lost, and why. Laudatory poems were allowed but no detailed official account of the voyage was published in England until nine years after the *Golden Hinde* returned, when it appeared in a book dedicated to the head of the Secret Service.

The length of that silence was the talk of Europe even at the time, and crucial aspects of the venture are still unknown. What was its purpose, even? The 'draft plan' for the voyage, discovered in 1929, tells us who the investors were and that this was intended as a journey of reconnaissance. Direct conflict with the Spanish was to be avoided. But the section which would have told us where the ships *were* meant to go has been burnt away. Some parts of the voyage are still impossible to trace accurately. How far south the ship went beyond Tierra del Fuego, or how far north along the coast of California his 'New Albion' was: these are still matters of conjecture.

Is the missing detail here a tell-tale sign of furtive state-sponsored burrowings? To each generation its own speculations. In our own time, the secrecy is often treated by historians as circumstantial evidence that Drake's intentions, and those of his backers, were legally dubious from the start. One source even suggests that Drake initially had instructions to deny that he had sailed around the world at all.

But what we don't know about Drake and his voyage is different from what we do know but have chosen to ignore or play down. We know, for example, from the deposition of his Portuguese pilot, Nuño da

Silva, that he carried 'a book in which he writes his log and paints birds, trees and seals. He is diligent in painting . . .'

We might assume that in this he was merely indulging a hobby or preparing to justify his later actions, but da Silva's words suggest something rather more committed. As chance would have it, we can actually see in some detail how the impression made by the natural world during this voyage was later ignored or played down.

—

And the 26 Sept . . . we safely with ioyfull minds and thankfull hearts to God, arrived at Plimoth, the place of our first set-ting forth, after we had spent 2 yeares 10 moneths and some few odde daies beside, in seeing the wonders of the Lord in the deep, in discouering so many admirable things, in going through with so many strange adventures, in escaping out of so many dangers, and ouercomming so many difficulties in this our encompassing of this neather globe, and passing round about the world, which we haue related.

So ends *The World Encompassed*, the first full-length account of the voyage, first published in 1628, nearly fifty years after the ship's return. Notice that it was 'in seeing the wonders of the Lord in the deep' that the list of their activities begins. Just for a moment sus-pend disbelief. It's quite possible that the man who wrote those words meant them quite literally.

The World Encompassed draws upon several sources but is mainly based, as the title page makes clear, on an account of the voyage by the expedition's chaplain, Francis Fletcher. Fletcher himself was unable to find a publisher for his manuscript but it was copied in the 1670s, illustrations included, 'the originall being exactly to a haire with this.' The original has disappeared but the first half of that copy survived.

A comparison of the text that was finally published with its main source tells us a lot about how the official narrative was arrived at. Fletcher, for example, is sceptical about the actions of 'the General' during the trial and execution of Thomas Doughty. Hence, presumably, Fletcher's difficulties in finding a publisher. Doughty, who styled himself a fellow-commander of the expedition, was tried as a traitor and a conjuror at Port St Julian, in what is now Argentina. Fletcher's views on this are simply absent from *The World Encompassed.* Drake's gangsterism, in other words, is endorsed by a deliberate down-playing.

But other aspects of the voyage have also been noticeably scaled back. As they head south towards the Equator from the Cape Verde Islands, for example, Fletcher observes that 'whereas Aristotle, Pythagoras, Thales, and many others, both Greekes and Latins, have taught that the *torrida zona* was not habitable . . . we proved the same to be altogeather false, and the same zone to be the earthly Paradise . . .' Nothing like this appears in the edited version.

The chaplain's relish for this 'earthly Paradise' shows nowhere more clearly than in his account of watching flying fish pursued by dolphins and tuna in mid-Atlantic:

Nature has taught them in their flying aloft to come downe head long to the water and glance their bodyes upon the upper surface of the water hereof to wett their winges, and to continue their flight as before, whereby they go scott free from their sea persecutors . . . many times they would flye against the toppe masts and sales of our ship, and against the bodyes of our men . . .

The flying fish do appear in *The World Encompassed* (one historian has referred to it as a 'digression about fish'). They make very little sense there because so much of the tone and colour of Fletcher's original observations has been painstakingly removed.

In the manuscript Fletcher's wonder at the newness of what he is seeing is palpable. The fry of the flying fish are described as 'being of the bignes of gnatts. They scudd upon the superficies of the water and skipp from place to place like grasshoppers'. Too decorative. Delete.

The greatest spoyle whereunto these flying fishes were subject to in the ayer, was that a multitude of strange birds did ever attend upon the shoales of dolphin and bonetta (tuna) in the ayer, knoweing that when they light upon the sholes of the flying fishes, they would put them up as a covey of partridges, and they presently as hawkes fell upon them, with all the violence to make havoke, and slew 1000 before they held one fast for their owne use, wherewith they pleasured their friends, the dolphins and bonettayes, in the sea, which received them with greedynes looking for more . . .

This is nature writing. 'In these and such pleasures,' Fletcher records, 'did we pass away 54 days' on the crossing from Cape Verde to Brazil. Note the first-person plural: Fletcher is not just speaking for himself. He records his discussions with the Portuguese pilot about what they were all seeing. It was his duty to 'Report such things of Gods great and marvailous works.' The islands they found off South America thick with penguins are sketched in a similarly rhapsodic, richly detailed style: 'some of them have upon their heads, standing upright, a little tuft of feathers like a peacock, and have red circles about their eyes which becom them well . . .'

They land on an island one evening to take some of the birds for food:

the night draweing on the fowles increased more & more so that there was no place for them to rest in. Nay ever third bird could not find anny roome in so much that they sought to settle themselves upon our heads shoulders arms & all parts of our body they could in most strange manner without anny feare . . .

'Penguin', meaning 'white head' in Welsh, originally referred to the now-extinct great auk. Fletcher was the first writer to use this term for the bird we still call by that name: 'Infinite were the Numbers of the foule which the Welch men name Pengwin.' They are still there in *The World Encompassed*, and they are still good for eating, but neither the enchantment nor the pathos have made it past the editor.

And we are surely justified in asking why. Dolphins and flying fish are admirable enough in their way, the official narrative seem to be saying. They will do for a bit of back-drop and extra protein. But any reaction they evoke as creatures in their own right is not reducible to financial, strategic or patriotic terms. Whatever anyone who was actually there may have thought, they are 'extraneous to the subject of the book.' They are irrelevant.

By drawing attention to this, I don't mean to suggest that this voyage, or any other 16th-century voyage, was some kind of wildlife cruise. The circumnavigation was certainly about statecraft and commerce. Those who invested in it made a 4700 per cent return on their investment. The Levant Company was set up using some of the money that was left over once Elizabeth had been able to pay off the entire national debt. And from the Levant Company there would one day emerge the East India Company.

But that is what the voyage meant for the English state and related business interests. The same state and the same related interests took care to manage the story about what it had meant from the moment Drake and his crew stepped ashore in Plymouth. This is part of a larger pattern. We still have the written 'instructions' on this from a follow-up voyage of 1582. They specify that all maps 'or descriptions of the said voyage' must be handed in to the commander when the ship returns and he in turn must pass these to the authorities. But nothing obliges us *now* to collude in this arrangement. The question about why those authorities needed to control the story so tightly matters more, ultimately, than the minutiae of where Drake went or even how much he stole.

It matters because consciously or otherwise the Age of Discovery in general, and the circumnavigation in particular, is still active in the way we see the wider world and our place in it. Over time this voyage has endured some very concerted attempts to force it into meaning two or three things and only those. It does not follow that those two or three things are *all* it meant.

ON WILDLIFE PHOTOGRAPHY

It isn't only the big historical narratives that suddenly look so fragile. This strange alteration reaches not only right around the world and back into our collective past, but into each of our own pasts, too. I must have been peripherally aware, during that run of bad winters in the late 1970s, of the larger debates around climate change. But I was twelve or so: those larger stories reached me heavily filtered through my pre-occupation with this or that particular creature.

I'd known at once that bird-watching was not about to go the way of all the other hobbies. My threadbare-green-jacket-with-field-glasses combination lent me new confidence. Spending most of the year away, it gave my 'home' community some ready idea of who I now thought I was. So this was helpful signage for all concerned. And landowners do expect to be asked. Most of the neighbouring farms I now began to call at were down long dirt tracks. Strange how I had to steel myself, heading down those unmetalled lanes at the start of each holiday, for all this asking of permission.

At the door they remained always a little on their guard behind those accents. With chapped hands much scrubbed at and weather-beaten faces, they listened, sceptical, with grey hair dishevelled and flattened from spending so much time under a cap day after day. What was he up to, this boy back from his boarding school?

The outfit was my new answer. Not that it allayed suspicions, exactly. Do not be concerned, it said, by early morning sightings of a teenager in green from top to toe, prowling the river-banks, lurking in field-corners. But tensions were already then building between farmers and 'conservationists'. Wasn't I perhaps checking their slurry overflow, their silage effluent? I was, surely, the kind who might.

It was only John Yelland who never gave me that look. What embarrassed me with him, rather, was how much he wanted to talk. I ought to have known loneliness when I saw it, but I didn't. He remembered when there were still red squirrels. Or it might be where had the salmon gone or about the otters he used to hear calling along the river most nights. His hair was silver now but he and his brother had been great egg-collectors once. He fidgeted nervously with the cloth cap as he told me their adventures, repeatedly lifting and fitting it back. He felt terrible about it now.

That his awkwardness was more than a match for my own also helped. He invited me in sometimes and from a shelf of accounting books took down once again the large plain wooden box. In each compartment of the several trays he lifted out sat an egg-shell on a wad of cotton wool. The label recorded in a tiny childish hand the species and the date of collection. They were mainly from two or three summers in the early 1940s.

To the young, the forgetfulness of the old is a mystery. And some of John's stories I'd heard many times. I treated seeing those eggs now and again as my reward for not showing my impatience. It was always the kingfisher eggs he wanted to show me especially. These were as luminously pale as they had ever been, ever since the day, as he invariably went on to confess, he and his brother had dug them out of the river-bank.

He invited me to marvel with him again at their strange and continuing whiteness. They needed to be so white to be visible to the parent birds in the dark chamber at the end of that tunnel. Or that's what he had read. What did I think? How rarely you see a kingfisher, or even hear one now, he went on, always apologising for the egg-collecting – knowing how it must make him look to this youngster. That it would class him, in my eyes, with the fox-hunters and hare-killers and all the rest of them.

Some of the other eggs had cracked. One or two had been reduced to little more than a pile of fragments nestled in the impression which the whole egg had once made in the cotton wool. The labels had been written by his brother, who had, I knew, as everyone knew, put a shot-gun in his mouth in the orchard where brambles had grown up since and the apples were no longer collected. He had wanted to marry the daughter in a family of labourers and his parents, humiliated by his choice, had refused permission.

With what manner of long-drawn-out grieving process I had to do, in my friendship with John, I shall never know. I was twelve or thirteen and mainly interested in bird-watching. Whenever he took out that wooden box, though – even I noticed this much – his remorse at digging out those kingfisher eggs and anxiety about their present rarity were never far away.

And it was true: these eggs were in fact as close as I'd ever got to one. Kingfishers had indeed become very rare. And this is what I mean about the impact of this new fragility on our own pasts. Sensitive to the cold, they'd been badly hit by several hard winters in a row and probably by pollution, too. I knew them the only way anyone could know them now: from books and the stories of old people.

The way he took their disappearance so personally both impressed and baffled me. To each generation its own diffuse sense of guilt. I could tell he always thought I was judging him. But I envied his egg-collecting far more than I judged it. Not for any freedom to vandalise that he may have enjoyed, but for his experience of a time 'before', when such wildlife could be taken for granted. For the assurance he had grown up with that it would always be there.

He could see, now, that he'd taken it too much for granted. He had used a dieldrin-based sheep-dip for years and in unguarded moments still marvelled at how well it had worked. Then he learnt, or chose to learn, too late, what the stuff was doing to river wildlife. But learning it, even too late, had changed him.

No subsidy ever tempted John to tear out his hedges. Not that he looked after them either. Riddled with rabbit-diggings, they had been broken down everywhere by his roving bands of extremely astute and half-wild sheep, famous for miles around. His hedges were, here and there, ineffectually patched with strands of barbed wire, bits of old iron bedstead or sheets of tin roofing, each marking the attempt to appease some irate neighbour. Years after everyone else had cleared them away, his farm was still crowded with elm skeletons – John left the wind to fell them in its own time. The wind was in no hurry.

I saw at the time what I wanted to see – namely, a nature reserve on my door-step. I can see now an ageing farmer with nobody to help. This amazing abundance of wildlife, which I welcomed as a bit of excellent luck, had much to do with tragic family circumstances. But what of that? Woodpeckers fluttered among the dead branches of the elms, feasting on all the grubs and larvae they went on supplying, year after year.

His fields lacked the queer emerald brilliance that had, with nitrate fertilisers, come over the pastures of his neighbours. He was not going to repeat his mistake with dieldrin. He had read about the effects of such fertiliser in the water system and so bought in slag from Welsh steel plants instead. He didn't buy in the new, faster-growing breeds of cattle, but kept the Devon reds he'd always reared.

He and his sisters arranged for me to give slide shows about local wildlife in the village hall, all proceeds to the church roof repairs. His being Church Warden was definitely a part of this. I know that biblically inflected sentimentalism about nature is as much out of fashion now as it was once in, and I know the reasons, but I am, indirectly, in its debt and should acknowledge that. It may have been assumed or hoped that I would eventually draw appropriate conclusions about a beneficent Creator.

People associate the countryside with nostalgia or

escapism and it's true, past and present are jumbled up differently there. But to me it always felt like a place where the real questions are much harder to dodge. Why had his brother done it? If this was a place where the older, better values had clung on, then what was it about those values that made people do something like that? I tried not to think about it every time I walked past that overgrown orchard. Or again, if pollution was killing off the rivers, that wasn't just some news item here. It meant derelict fishing huts where the anglers used to keep their rods. It meant hotel staff needing another job. Or it was something your slightly eccentric neighbour still could not forgive himself for.

—

I was sitting at a bend in the river one morning when out of nowhere came the wavering, whirring point of light, the orange glow and the inflammatory blue re-entering the river's atmosphere after their long absence. Skimming low over the pebbles and the water, they announced a restoration of the old plenty, in a voice all made up of dots and dashes and exclamation marks.

And I saw in a flash what the fuss, what those eggs and stories, had been about. Kingfishers were soon re-established and a regular sight once more. The warming trend of which this return was a symptom was not exactly what I took it for at the time. I saw what I wanted to: this improved weather was a 'correction' of what had gone before. So much for what we all imagined back then. But they were back: I had time to watch more carefully and they had time to start resembling more closely what I was familiar with from bird books. It took me a year or two to think of some way to mark their reappearance.

I'd bought a camera meanwhile. Where an alder torn out of the bank had become lodged in the riverbed, it lay on its side and went on sprouting leaves as floods piled a shingly island around it. More than once, I'd spied a kingfisher gleaming among those branches laid horizontally over the water. I asked John if I could set up my canvas hide on his river-bank. I didn't tell him exactly why. I needed a measure of secrecy to contact these creatures for myself.

Having set the hide up I left it empty for a day or two. I had no sooner occupied it than I realised that the fallen tree I had taken for their 'fishing-post' was really just a perch from which the parents glanced around before the final dash to the nest-burrow. I actually had to see an adult bird dive head-first into the sandy river-bank and disappear completely before I got it. It had never even crossed my mind that this could happen on my own little stretch of river. I wondered if this was the very river-bank from which the two brothers had removed kingfisher eggs forty years before? By now they were a protected species: to set up my hide this close to a nest was not, in the eyes of the law, that much better than digging out its contents.

But I was in no hurry to take it down and I soon realised something else too, or rather the birds did. My hide had made their previous look-out superfluous and was quickly adopted as a better alternative. So instead of having them perch a few convenient feet away, I would hear wings and then that piercing whistle very very close. The stretched green canvas would tremble, then tighten fractionally and I knew that a kingfisher was sitting an inch or two from my head.

To peer out at the passing river and know myself in such brilliant company might be its own reward but I was holding out for that photograph. In even moderately fine weather, I happily half-suffocated that summer away in my green canvas cube. And eventually four fledglings, one hazy afternoon, fluttered down to a ledge above the water. They practised hawking after the pond-skaters which gathered where the current ran sluggishly along the bank.

One of the young birds did eventually take up position on the perch I had arranged for them. That was the photograph I gave John in a frame as a Christmas card. The old abundance is back, was what I meant by it. Whether he knew, or would have agreed, I can't say. The next time he invited me in it was on his mantelpiece. Did it allay that conscience of his? I never asked.

Meanwhile I had taken my course of free lessons in motionless river-watching, given by a pair of resident kingfishers. I'd watched how the young ones dashed clumsily at the water, too, plunging and dunking, madly rushing in at the wrong angle, again and again, crash-landing and bobbing back up. Time after time I watched the way they shook themselves off after each attempt, then fluttered back to the ledge and went straight back to darting after those hapless pondskaters, pursuing them this way and that. They weren't bad teachers, either.

I took fewer and fewer photographs after this and I'm still not sure about most of what passes for 'wildlife photography'. I don't only mean that it is so much easier to collect such images now. I mean it feels symptomatic to me of how impersonal our relations with the natural world have become.

Even as we close down so much of what these creatures depend on, so our images of them multiply. And wildlife photography is, essentially, a rolling advertisement for this state of affairs. So much crisp focus, so many perfectly framed shots. How rarely it even aims to communicate some developing relationship with the creature. Still more rarely does it speak of a relationship which more than one person might share with a given creature over time, or of how a wild creature, even by disappearing for a while, can mediate between people and between generations, too.

THE PARADOXAL COMPASS

1580 May 17th, at the Moscovy house for the Cathay voyage. June 3rd, Mr A.Gilbert and J. Davys rod homeward into Devonshire.

– from John Dee's Diary

My second year at university was over but I did not ride homeward into Devonshire. I was fine where I was. In a small room at the end of a complicated corridor I stayed on as the college switched from organising its annual May Ball to catering for conference delegates. The trees and fields where the colleges back onto the river belonged to tourism again. Only a few days into the vacation, it was as if the magnums and marquees and ball gowns had never been.

Social Cambridge was an enigma and remained so to the end. The 'social side' to college life was, in the mid-late Eighties, triumphalist. I tended to get on better with foreign students. Or maybe I protest too much. Perhaps growing up down a lane was ideal for watching kingfishers or herons and good for reading too, but turned out not to be much of a preparation for the 'social side'.

For whatever reason it felt unaccountably good to be here, alone, thinking and reading. I was going to Rome for the first time later in the summer and that room was the best place I could think of to prepare for it. The college also gave each second-year student £40 to buy any books they liked. I've often thought since what a good idea that was.

None of the titles I'd chosen had much to do with coursework. But I had gone on reading about the explorers and one of the books I chose was partially to do with that. What interested me now, more than their adventures in themselves, were the motives of those who sent them out. *Why* they went. So I'd bought a biography of the Renaissance polymath, and founding fellow of my college, John Dee.

Dee was mathematical adviser to the Muscovy Company and as such the instructor of both John Davis and Stephen Borough. His home in Mortlake, on the banks of the Thames, operated as a kind of independent research institute. Indeed, John Davis seems to have spent some part of his upbringing there. This *hospitali philosophorum peregrinatum,* or 'hostelry for wandering philosophers', housed '4 or 5 rooms full of books' (then the largest library in the country) as well as globes, quadrants, and three 'laboratories'.

Nobody agrees about anything to do with Dee, which is part of what recommended him to me. To some historians he is little more than a delusional magician, a meddling peripheral. To others he is the outstanding teacher of his age. It's certainly true that many of the most distinguished mathematicians of the following generation had been his pupils, John Harriot and Thomas Digges among them.

Dee is the perfect introduction to just how strange

the English Renaissance was. Court-intriguer, Greek scholar and metallurgical adviser to the government. A lawyer and an authority on all things Welsh, an all-purpose political advisor and a necromancer. Read about Dee and it soon becomes clear the purpose of these voyages was as complicated as the age in which he lived. But every subsequent generation has had to discover that purpose afresh. What was manifestly heroic to Kingsley was manifestly tawdry and grasping a century later.

Above all, Dee was ardent in the cause of what he himself called 'this British discovery and recovery enterprise'. One of his proudest achievements – he was still boasting about it twenty years later – was the 'Paradoxal Compass', which he designed in the year of Stephen Borough's first voyage to the Arctic. The 'Compass' itself has not survived and there is more than one theory about what it was. He was unable to raise enough money to publish the book which contained his own explanation and the manuscript is now lost.

It was probably a circumpolar chart rather than an actual 'compass', offering a view of the earth with the North Pole at its centre. This would have distorted the shapes of countries in higher latitudes less than the Mercator projection. He may have called it a 'compass' because, unlike most charts, it was round, with meridians radiating from its centre, like the lines on a compass. It was 'paradoxal' because a course which would have been drawn as a straight line on a plane chart appeared as a spiral on this new kind of chart.

It attempted, in other words, to translate the earth's curved surface onto a flat chart as this had never been attempted before. He had found the way to represent a world about which people suddenly knew both more and less than ever before. Its invention may well have been prompted by studying one of the globes which he is known to have brought back to Cambridge from Louvain in 1547. They, too, have since been lost but perhaps some trace of them haunts those buildings yet. Perhaps that was why I felt so well reading about them in that little room at the end of a complicated corridor.

The Paradoxal Compass would have accompanied Borough on his first and on subsequent journeys. Was its invention a *purely* technical feat? Dee would have denied it. It was a 'law of nature', he wrote, which offered his contemporaries 'the whole Ball & Sphericall frame of the erth & water.' But this 'law' required in return that they 'be to the Omnipotent Creator, sincerely thankfull & to the humayn society, friendly & comfortable.' We might be inclined to dismiss that as pious window-dressing, particularly in view of what actually then happened, but are we justified in reading that kind of cynicism about religious language into 16th-century motives?

From the original of Shakespeare's Prospero to Derek Jarman's punk magus to Iain Sinclair's psychogeographical super-phantom, from the arch-conjuror of Glynn Parry's biography to Damon Albarn's recent rock opera, Dee goes on and on. If something about him continues to appeal, perhaps it's the way he struggled to integrate the traumatic changes his society was undergoing. The way he marshalled every possible language – scientific, economic, religious, alchemical, political – at a time when none of these was fully distinct from any of the others, in his efforts to forge a new coherence.

As Stephen Borough guided England's search for a route to China, it was Dee's 'law of Nature' he applied, following that Arctic shoreline in the *Searchthrift*. John Davis in his turn applied the same, from Scilly to Greenland and back again. The English navigators seeking a way to Asia via the far north were certainly following the money. They were also seeking to avoid competition with Spanish and Portuguese rivals. But to reduce what they were doing to its economic and strategic aspects is certainly to misrepresent it.

By navigation, Dee had written in his Preface to Euclid (1570), 'might growe Commoditye, to this land chiefly, and to the rest of the Christen Common wealth, farre passing all riches and earthly Threasure.' A commodity far passing all riches and earthly treasure. This enigmatic phrase has given rise to much speculation. It may be a coded reference to the elixir of life, which alchemical tradition had long claimed was to be found in China. T'ang Dynasty magicians did indeed claim to have found the recipe.

Whatever Dee's mysterious 'commodity' is a reference to, the navigators were certainly sent out for many reasons other than the collapsing price of woollen cloth and a weakening currency. The earliest mention of Davis anywhere is in John Dee's diary. But the diary remains silent on the exact purpose of his visit, as it does with the vast majority of other such visits. Dee had cast the Queen's horoscope: the explorers and their backers were as likely to have been consulting him on an astrologically favourable date for their expeditions as for advice on navigation. Generally, we have no way of knowing which, or whether it was both or something else entirely. Such was the nature of the age.

But when Davis refers to Dee's Paradoxal Compass as one of the instruments 'necessary for a skilfull Seaman', he is clearly referring to its practical usefulness. It permitted sea captains to sail in high latitudes with greater confidence than ever before. There were several reasons why greater confidence was needed, why navigation in the far north presented new difficulties.

Quite aside from the quantity of ice they found in their way, attempting to reach China by a northern route forced the English to deal with magnetic variation. This is the difference between the magnetic 'north', which a compass-needle points to, and polar north, the fixed point on a map. That this difference exists had been noticed by Columbus, and by the Chinese long before that, but it has relatively little effect in lower latitudes.

In higher latitudes understanding how variation works is essential because the effect is so much larger. Variation was explained in different ways. Some thought the compass needle was controlled by a celestial body – a star in the tail of Ursa Major was one suggestion. Others assumed a magnetic mountain must be responsible, or a magnetic island, perhaps, somewhere north of Siberia.

The people who knew most about this problem in 16th-century England were either people who had been on that first expedition to the Arctic or had been associated with it. One of the first books dedicated to the subject was written by William Borough, another pupil of John Dee's, also of Borough Farm, Northam, who had, aged seventeen, accompanied his elder brother Stephen on that first voyage to Russia.

William's *Discours of the Variation* appeared in 1581, bound together with a book by his compass-maker, Robert Norman. Borough wrote as an experienced navigator, not a cosmologist. It is a thoroughly practical account of the question that he gives. Only by repeated observation, by the methodical logging and comparison of data, could earlier faults be identified and corrected. It is in such writings that we can see a new view of the world emerging.

And a new kind of pride with it. The inaccurate charting of a coast was a sign of 'unskilful sea-men', a mark of national slovenliness. Any mariner deserving the name should be able to chart 'the banks, rocks and sholds in the sea, with the depths & other necessary notes obserued in his owne trauails [travels]' and do so 'according vnto the truth (which is the chiefest part required in a perfect mariner.)'

William instructed other mariners in the use of the Paradoxal Compass and rose to high office in the Navy Board, also succeeding his older brother as Chief Pilot to the Muscovy Company. He is credited with having discovered the log and line method of measuring a ship's progress and once declared bullishly that he needed nothing more to sail around the world than a compass and a plain chart. Yet he was a meticulous master of the new navigational art. His determination to record variation as precisely as possible, would have, as we shall see, consequences far beyond anything he could have anticipated.

A month after Drake returned from the circumnavigation, Borough carefully measured the magnetic variation from Limehouse, in London. Less than a mile away, a special dry dock was being built around the *Golden Hinde* at Deptford, where the ship soon settled into its new career as a tourist attraction. Borough's book on magnetic variation appeared a year to the day after Drake's return. In it, Borough urges both 'the vulgar and learned sort' to 'seek knowledge in Arithmatique & Geometry.'

Borough had a near-identical background to Drake and clearly recognised his genius. In his account of the ideal seaman as explorer and map maker, he praised his fellow West Countryman, who 'for valorous attempt, prudent proceeding & fortunate performing his voyage about the world, is not onely become equall to any [seamen] that liue, but in fame farre surmounteth them all.' It is as a *navigator* that Drake is praised. But 'prudent proceeding & fortunate performing' surely carries sardonic undertones. There was indeed trouble ahead.

Before we come to that, Borough's references to the Scilly Isles are also revealing. For him they are above all a navigational aid, helpful in studying magnetic variation. Close to the 50th parallel north, they provided a convenient sightline for any English ship *en route* to the New World. He observed that on the charts used by trawler captains 'the course is set downe from Sillie to Capo Raso' (now Cape Race, Labrador). This interested him because he knew Cape Race is in fact more than three degrees to the south of Scilly. It suggested that English compasses, adjusted for magnetic variation as it was in England, became misleading as the ship travelled west.

Borough will already in his teens have been aware that the variation, as measured from London and Northern Russia, was wildly inconsistent. Later expeditions to Labrador, to which he was an advisor, only confirmed what the Newfoundland fishermen had already told him. Borough observes this 'strange variety' and publishes it to the world, perhaps with a hint of mockery, 'to the end that the learned sort might consider thereof, and sharpening their wits, see what probable causes & grounds they can assign for the same.'

Here, then, is a contradictory figure: technically expert yet wary of 'the learned sort', well versed in the science but with a deep respect, also, for the knowledge of 'ordinary' seamen. You might think, along with the West Country background, that this would have made Drake and Borough the firmest of friends. Yet six years after the appearance of his *Discours of the Variation*, they dragged each other through a bruising court case.

After the successful raid which Drake had led on Cadiz, Borough had declined to play any part in the assault on a smaller Portuguese settlement and stood accused of cowardice. Drake hoped to use the town as a base from which to take prizes. The same settlement, Sagres, on Cape St Vincent, had been a centre for the earliest developments anywhere in navigational science. Borough would certainly have been aware of these associations, whether or not he had accompanied his elder brother to Seville as a young man.

I do not mean here to seek out hate-figures and pit them against heroes, or vice versa. Drake and both of the Boroughs, Dee and Davis too, were thoroughly men of their own times. They believed in divine missions, fell out among themselves, committed preposterous errors of judgement and sometimes paid for them. They were committed imperialists, fully intent upon civilising the savages. They did not, in other words, distinguish in the same way as we would between the better and worse applications of the new knowledge. But it is nevertheless clear from their writings, and from those of people closely associated with them, that they did make a distinction of some kind.

PART TWO

– Questions Emerge –

PERVERSE AND QUIBBLING HERETICS

They sail over the oceans. I've nothing against that – but they put their faith in a brass ball called a compass, not in God.
– The Inquisitor in Brecht's *The Life of Galileo*

Already in 1581, doubts about the recently returned 'golden knight' were widespread. Drake offered treasure to Burghley and to others and was rebuffed. Given Drake's immense wealth and popularity – and on occasion his temper – it is unsurprising that criticisms were muted. Nor perhaps that the most eloquent expression of concern has been overlooked. It is to be found in the preface to Robert Norman's *The Newe Attractive*, the book which was bound together with William Borough's *Discours of the Variation*. Norman, Borough's compass-maker, warmly thanks his friend who 'first gave occasion that I fell into consideration of this question' and 'through whose encouragement I entered further into examination of the matter.'

The Newe Attractive was one of the first purely scientific texts ever written – it is regarded by some as the very first. But it opens with a poem, 'The Loadstone's Challenge', about the purpose of this new knowledge.

A 'lodestone' was a piece of heavy black stone which was used to re-magnetise the needle in a ship's compass. A form of iron oxide known today as 'magnetite', in this poem it challenges in turn the diamond, the ruby and the sapphire to justify their popularity. They would, the lodestone argues, all be lying at the bottom of 'Indian seas' were it not for his, the lodestone's virtue. 'I guide the Pilat's course, / his helping hand am I, / The Mariner delights in me, / so doth the merchant man. / My vertu lies unknowen, / my secretes hidden are . . .' He calls upon his flashy rivals to 'blush then' and acknowledge him 'the prince of stones alone.' Merchant and mariner each respond to this challenge, confessing themselves persuaded: 'the loadstone is the stone / the onely stone alone . . .'

The verse may be jaunty enough but there is a serious point to it, as to the text that follows. The safety of mariners and security of trade routes all depend, this poem argues, on the expert use of something not outwardly glamorous at all. It was only by means of this black pebble that a ship could constantly re-charge its sense of direction. Norman, like Borough, treated navigation as an engrossing science, both fascinating in itself and practically useful. Both he and Borough were artisans or technicians, new men. There are defensive disclaimers about a lack of formal education before he goes straight to the heart of the matter.

The ancients before him, Pythagoras, Archimedes and others, were:

carried and ouercome wyth the incredible delight conceiued of their own deuices and inuentions, though they followe partly the peculiar contentation of their priuat fancies, yet they seme chiefly to respect either the glorie of god or the furtheraunce of some public commoditie. Whose good example in this behalf I will indeuour to followe . . . seeing it hath pleased God to make me the instrument to open thys Noble secret, that his name might be glorified, and the commoditie of my Country procured thereby.

The 'incredible delight' of exercising the power of invention had given us the art of navigation and this art had, in turn, made the English 'Citizens of the worlde'. All the arguments in this book were grounded 'onely upon experience, reason and demonstration.' Norman's work is informed throughout both by the new scientific rigour and by the excitement of a great collaborative venture.

He is keenly aware, too, that these breakthroughs are without precedent. As the lodestone offered practical guidance so its properties hint also at 'Noble secrets' only now being investigated. *The Newe Attractive* will 'set downe a late experimented truth found in this stone', will reveal a state of understanding greater than that of any ancient authority. He will show that the world is on the brink of a new kind of understanding, about to take us beyond anything dreamed of by the ancients.

Norman would later expand on his hopes for this emergent discipline. Through navigation 'we learn the situations, natures, customes and dealings of other countries,' he wrote. Through trade 'the need that one man hath for another more cleerely appeareth.' The new learning, then, is no license to plunder. In taking rubies and sapphires down a peg, his poem unmistakably suggests that alongside such advances in knowledge, the allure of precious stones is not just a little prosaic. It is downright shallow. Other stones are dismissed as 'glittering sparks' that should give way to the outwardly humbler lodestone.

This is why it should be regarded as the prince of stones. And this is published a year to the day after Drake's acclaimed and treasure-laden return, by a figure well known to and highly respected by the community of navigators. One of Dee's closest associates, Adrian Gilbert, owned lodestone mines and the metal is known to have been quarried in Devon, too: these might not have quite the same hold over the public imagination as the silver mines of Potosi or the city of El Dorado, or Philip's galleons, for that matter, but perhaps, the poem suggests, they should.

—

Around the time that Norman's book appeared, the Queen's physician, William Gilbert, began to develop and test a theory of his own. It was Gilbert who gave us the word 'electricity', but his theory was about magnetism. What if it was not stars or mountains or islands that were responsible for the magnetic field, he asked.

What if the earth itself were a magnetically charged sphere, its vast body animated by a magnetic soul? Like Borough and Norman, he was determined that his theory should be backed by solid evidence. Over almost twenty years he sought out anyone who could offer practical insight into how magnetism worked. And the best-informed group he could possibly ask about it were, of course, mariners.

Gilbert followed up on William Borough's earlier investigations. He boasts of information about compass behaviour in the southern hemisphere 'pointed out to me and confirmed by our most illustrious Neptune, Francis Drake.' But he was particularly curious about observations taken by navigators following the 50th parallel 'from the Scilly Isles bound for Newfoundland.' The book he finally published in 1600, *De Magnete*, or *On the Magnet*, was the only book he ever wrote. It made him famous all over Europe.

Johannes Kepler, for one, rated Gilbert as one of the three chief architects of the astronomical revolution, along with Copernicus and Tycho. Kepler even wrote from Venice to tell him so and recommended *De Magnete* to the man who would be its most sophisticated reader, Galileo Galilei. The greatest astronomer of his age became convinced he had found in Gilbert's work the physics to back up Copernican mathematics. Magnetism it must be that caused the planets to spin on their axes and magnetism, pervading the universe, shaped their orbits, too.

Galileo could not praise Gilbert too highly. In the book for which he would be tried by the Inquisition, his *Dialogue Concerning the Two Chief World Systems*, he has 'the highest praise, admiration and envy' for Gilbert. He does not doubt that 'in the course of time this new science will be improved with still further observations', but this 'need not diminish the glory of the first observer'. He compares Gilbert's power of insight with those of Pythagoras and approves of the divine status which the Greeks accorded to their greatest inventors.

Recall Robert Norman's determination to emulate the Greeks in the delight they had found in invention. Norman had, intriguingly, drawn just the same parallel between the 'point' of scientific breakthroughs now and what they had meant to the ancients. He, too, singled out Pythagoras' joy at discovering his geometric laws.

Galileo wrote that Gilbert's book had led him to 'a realisation that numberless things in nature remain unknown to the human intellect', and yet what science was uncovering was 'not a new thing, but as ancient as the earth itself.' Compare the sentiments expressed in Norman's poem about the lodestone and Galileo's excitement: 'It seems to me,' says one of the characters in his *Dialogue*, 'that this stone [the lodestone] opens to the human mind a large field for philosophising . . .'

When Galileo referred to his own system as 'the Pythagorean philosophy' his readers knew that

'Pythagorean' was code for believing that the earth went round the sun. The Greeks had speculated about this possibility two thousand years earlier. When Galileo mocks the 'slavery to one particular writer or another' from which Gilbert's approach has liberated him, it is a whole world view he is, implicitly, threatening. Of the Inquisition's four proofs of Galileo's guilt, one was that he 'cites approvingly the opinions of William Gilbert, a perverse and quibbling heretic.'

That 50th parallel passing just to the north of the Scillies might be extended, then, and re-figured as a liquid line connecting the Newfoundland boats and the Boroughs to William Gilbert and Galileo Galilei and everything that followed from him. Why do we not more often situate the explorers somewhere on that line? To do so is not to whitewash them. Nobody could argue with Drake's skill, but, as we've seen, there were those who did find ways to question or oppose the way he used it.

How well have we been served by the cult of the cut-throat sea dog? Has it provided us with a useable, grown-up account of these people and the astonishing time through which they lived? One of the first things Drake did upon entering the Pacific was to observe a lunar eclipse. He supplied readings of magnetic variation in the southern hemisphere to a researcher, who in turn became one of the major influences on Galileo Galilei. He discovered open sea to the south of Tierra del Fuego. He did not, of course, any more than Davis did, find open water to the north of North America, but he does seem to have looked for it. To sum up the purpose of this voyage as a 'pirate expedition' will not do.

—

The object of veneration, a cracked, dull disk, seems a little lost amidst all the celebrations in its honour. It peers dimly from a riot of foliage and ribbons and scientific instruments, all carved in ivory. The inscription reads: 'The sky opened by the lynx-like thought of Galileo, with this first glass lens he showed stars never seen before...' The relic, in other words, is the lens through which Jupiter's moons were first observed. They were moving and they were definitely not orbiting the earth. They were therefore breaking an elementary rule of an astronomical system which had seemed to work for two thousand years.

Galileo named these planets after Cosimo de' Medici, Grand Duke of Florence, and gave him the lens he had seen them through. It is still kept in Florence and I went to see it there on my way down to Rome. Through the account it gives of Galileo, each generation writes anew what the Renaissance and what meaningful dissent have come to mean. His story is an inexhaustible resource. His clarity and courage, but his recantation, too, still hold a terrible fascination.

He was no plaster saint – that pseudo-reliquary in Florence really gets him completely wrong – but I was looking in the right place at least. Bertolt Brecht wrote *The Life of Galileo* in 1940 as an exile from Nazi Germany. His Galileo was a 'believer in the gentle power of reason over men' and a believer too in the liberating power of the new knowledge. 'If you want to find the true greatness of ancient Greece, that mighty spirit of enquiry, alive today, go to the shipyards,' his Galileo enthuses. 'In the rope and sail shops five hundred hands move in the harmony of a new scheme of things.' And it's clear from his *Dialogue* that the real Galileo did follow Gilbert's and Borough's example in questioning mariners about their experiences of navigation.

For Brecht that 'power of reason', that 'new scheme of things', which his homeland had so fatefully betrayed, was socialism. A decade later, with the nuclear stand-off between the Cold War superpowers underway, Albert Einstein saw it rather as a question of authority and how it is generated. 'The *leitmotiv* which I recognise in Galileo's work is the passionate fight against any kind of dogma based on authority... Actually we are not so far removed from such a situation as we might like to flatter ourselves,' he wrote in 1952, as hysteria in his adopted homeland over 'Communist subversives' was wound up to a new pitch.

The version of Brecht's play which I read as a student was still addressing an irrationalism as political as it was scientific. 'The Cold War . . . grips minds and distorts reality more fiercely than ever,' wrote the playwright Howard Brenton in 1980, in his translator's note. 'That betrayal three hundred and fifty years ago is still with us . . . this is a desperately timely play.' He likened the smuggling of Galileo's last work out of Italy, with which the play ends, to the smuggling of dissident literature out of communist Eastern Europe.

And the play's timeliness did not cease with the passing of the Cold War order. When Galileo inveighs against the authorities who 'hide their machinations from the people by keeping them in a narcotic haze of superstition and old words', when his lens-grinder inveighs against the great families 'who order the earth to be still so their castles don't come tumbling down,' this story seems as 'desperately timely' as ever it was.

His iron founder, in Brecht's version, praises him as 'a man fighting for the freedom to teach new things.' And so he was. But he was fighting to teach old things a new way, also. Of this Brecht and Brenton between them offer only sly hints. For them his allusions to religion must be ironic. But the Galileo who gave us his interpretation of Psalm 19 was not laughing up his sleeve.

'The heavens declare the glory of God; and the firmament showeth his handiwork,' it begins. Verse 5, in the version Galileo would have known, reads: *in sole posuit tabernaculum suum*, in the sun He (God) has placed his tabernacle. Such 'imaginative' elements may look uninteresting to us, but no account of how modern science came about is complete without them.

If, Galileo argued, the sun is a tabernacle *for* the power of God, then the heat and light which radiate *from* the sun and circulate through the universe, are manifestations of His divine power. When, therefore, in the next verse, the sun is described as being like a 'bridegroom coming out of his chamber', rejoicing 'as a strong man to run a race', it is the heat and light of solar energy – and the life they bring – which are being described as God-like, not the sun itself.

Galileo was a close reader, too, of the Greek philosophers, Philolaus in particular, who had argued that the earth revolved around the centre of the universe, imagined as a central fire. He combined, in other words, his sense of the new science's potential, with close reading and nuanced interpretation of biblical scripture and ancient philosophy alike.

He taught old things a new way because he was riven by the contradictions of his own age. The trial and the recantation, the life under house arrest, all of these came about because something in those contradictions singled Galileo out as the one who must be made an example of. But he himself was not immune from what seems so paradoxical to us about that age. That is why his example, his bravery, retain their fascination. That is why he is the dissenter who still matters.

A WINTER RENTAL

Portland extends four miles out into the English Channel. A graduate of no fixed abode, I caught a bus onto 'the island' one cold night at the end of 1991. In the one-bedroom stone cottage which I found there, I was going to write about the collapse of Communism as I'd witnessed it. I wanted to set down my thoughts, now that the threat of nuclear war was past, about what that threat had meant while I was growing up with it and what its withdrawal meant now. The theme was too abstract and I was much too churned up by all the aftermath to get any perspective on it. The Soviet Union had just gone and Yugoslavia was about to blow. Iraq had already happened. Even as I tried to write, I could feel my idea being superseded by events. It was something else that captured my attention that winter.

I knew I was supposed to be 'getting into the media'. That, of course, is what an arts degree from a top university is for. Something about my recent experiences seemed the obvious place to start. But having travelled and worked in formerly communist countries, I'd noted how few of Eastern Europe's dissidents were journalists. Partly that was because the media under Communism was state-run and therefore simply not available as an outlet for the more scrupulous kind of writer.

So it was to philosophers and novelists, to playwrights and scholars and poets that you had to go, if you wanted to find out what the opponents of Communism had actually been saying. And I was haunted, as I read, by a new and uneasy feeling. One consequence of the collapse of the Berlin Wall was that the surface area of my ignorance had just doubled in size. I wonder if other Western Europeans weren't similarly daunted to discover suddenly how much they did not know. Isn't that a part of why some people now resent the easterners so much? They make us feel ignorant. And we are.

The dissidents were already yesterday's news but there was something about them I was only noticing now and couldn't get enough of. As long as the Western media paid them any attention it was as 'our' advance guard. These had been the risk-takers, or, rather, the guys who were now vindicated through having been on our side all along.

But when you read them, they weren't like that. They were a varied lot but very much the kind of people who would, in this country, have been dismissed as hippies or ignored as academics. They were intellectuals, misfits. A cottage towards the southern end of Portland was just the sort of place people like that would have ended up here, listening to the wind in a stone chimney. It was true that they had opposed the Communists – for which they had often paid dearly – but their 'anti-Communism' was, just as often, highly sceptical of what the West so rapidly set about replacing Communism with.

In Russia, the physicist Andrei Sakharov was already in the 1960s warning about the impact upon the climate of continuing to burn coal. He would become one of the Soviet Union's fiercest critics. In East Germany the first 'Environmental Library' (*Umweltbibliothek*) was established in 1986 and found a welcome in the basement of a Lutheran parish office in Berlin. It published a magazine called 'Environmental Pages' (*Umweltblätter*), which concerned itself with the impact of burning (and mining) brown coal as well as human rights and global poverty. When the Stasi arrested and detained the people who were running it, this triggered country-wide protests in 1987, the first of the wave of unrest which led ultimately to the mass demonstrations of 1989.

One of the finest expressions of the Czech dissenting spirit, Václav Havel's 'Politics and Conscience', took our collective mistreatment of the environment as its starting point. In Hungary, opposition to the construction of a nuclear power station on the Danube triggered wider protests against Communist rule. The appearance of a WWF calendar in 1989, the so-called 'otter calendar', made an impression which is still fondly recalled today. In Bulgaria, the Chernobyl cloud and the Soviet state which had lied about it were central to the growing concern about how the country was governed.

It is surely striking, with hindsight, how concerned these people already were with questions of energy generation. Yet westerners remain largely unaware of the role the environment played in the undermining of Communist rule in Eastern Europe. This isn't the story the winners chose to tell, although they could have. Indeed, had they chosen to, Europe might not have found itself in its current fix, because it would have set itself more meaningful goals than malls and motorways, more cake forever. It wasn't the story western companies with their 'logical growth strategies' wanted to hear, so nobody heard it. Even easterners rarely seem to be aware of the role environmentalism played in their 'liberation'.

A writer like Jan Patočka, for example, mentor to Havel and many others, did not oppose Communism with hopes of the 'other' system's victory. He countered it, rather, with the awareness of a thoroughgoing crisis of human identity to which Soviet communism was plainly inadequate. Capitalism, for its part, only swamped what communism stifled. Each might loudly proclaim its superiority and each had armed itself to the teeth in its own defence. To this my surroundings (Portland was still then home to a Navy base) bore eloquent testimony. But neither system was able to resolve that deeper crisis of human identity of which both were symptoms.

Dissidents of this kind were sceptical from the start, in other words, about the 'free market'. Their message, in so far as they had one, was less Coca-Cola® than *a plague o' both your houses*. After their invasion of Czechoslovakia in 1968, the Russians had hoped to stifle further unrest by introducing their own cut-price version of consumerism, so the blandishments of bad TV and the rest were not entirely new. For some the western 'package' – elections every four or five years plus cool stuff for the lucky ones and entertainment for everybody – was arguably worse than Communism. All that package did was disguise the underlying crisis more efficiently.

But what intrigued me most was that wars, for Patočka, were no longer discrete events with a beginning and an end. 'The contempt for life, the same poisons of suspicion, slander and demagoguery spread everywhere' and are deployed, just as they are in war, 'in order to drive [the enemy] to an inner collapse serving one's own interests.' War, as he put it, 'has insidiously changed form without coming to an end.' Ten thousand terrible films attest to our helpless fascination with it. But our everyday lives, too, he argued, have been recreated in the image of a 'savage liberty'. The single-minded pursuit of one's own interests, together with the deliberate undermining of anyone who is in the way – these are expressions of the same principle. These qualities are what we truly admire in people and our culture of consumption no longer makes any effort to conceal it.

—

The Centimetric Early Warning Radar Station was built next to one of Portland's prisons in the 1950s.

It was designed to track incoming missiles and the guardhouse was built in local stone in an effort to disguise the whole facility as a kind of posh bungalow. The control room, seventy feet below the surface, was reached by a lift. Those tarmac oblongs all around are long-vacant radar plinths. Missile technology moved on and the station was obsolete within a few years. By the time I got there the area was being used to train the dogs which patrol military airfields and other installations.

The Cold War might be over, but if peace had broken out you would hardly have guessed it on Portland. Military helicopters descending into HMS Osprey swung in over Chesil Beach as alarmingly low as ever. The concrete stanchions and wire fencing around the Admiralty research facilities remained firmly in place. Submarines and warships went on arriving and departing.

So did wars not really end anymore? Was Patočka right? On one ramble, I happened upon the Naval cemetery and noticed how many of the headstones had been set up not during conflicts but in the intervals between them. Accidents or deaths from injuries received in wartime, I supposed, and left it at that.

But I know now others shared the Czech's intuition about this, and not only to the east. Theodor Adorno, a German émigré in America, had been similarly unconvinced by the end of the Second World War: 'The idea that after this war life will continue normally or even that culture might be "re-built" . . . is idiotic . . . Is it conceivable . . . that the quantity of victims will not be transformed into a new quality of society at large, barbarism?'

For others, the machine which had been built to win in Europe and the Pacific was on such a scale that it would never voluntarily dismantle itself. Paul Goodman in New York suspected as much even before it was over – war, as he put it, was now 'for the duration'. Of this the Vietnam War seemed to him, as to many other Americans, further confirmation. And the evidence is still accumulating. Current fixations on the Second World War, particularly in Britain and Russia, are surely symptoms of the same condition.

But Patočka was saying both this and something slightly different: that no matter how the system we live under officially describes itself, the military machine is an expression of a deeper destructiveness about modern humans, both in relation to each other and to the world around them. 'Peace', as we understand it, based on over-consumption, was for him better described as 'demobilisation', because it can only issue in further wars over the resources which make that consumption possible. The war is for the duration *because* our common war against the earth never lets up.

—

Portland was not short on confirmations of this pessimistic theory. The top of the island is a vast messy workshop, a landscape of spoil-heaps and back-fill and stock-piled blocks. Much of its surface is a jumble of loose rubble terraces, bulldozed into position once the valuable underlying 'freestone' has been removed. I remember the siren which eerily preceded the sound of blasting back then. This place was plenty sombre enough for a twenty-something with a lot on his mind.

Much of its coastline is still littered with boulders or rough-cut blocks, among which post-industrial, un-employed-looking foxes still glide gingerly around in the middle of the afternoon. Ravens and falcons scrape some kind of a living amidst the brokenness. I gather the spoil-heaps and abandoned quarries are home to other survivals. Information boards palm this off on the gullible as 'wildlife'.

My point is you don't need to travel for this. Our engagement with the natural world right here is war-zone enough, all be it for a different kind of correspondent. You do need to know some background for this one, but then that is true of any conflict. It is through centuries of furnishing the official culture with what it required that this island has been steadily degraded.

By later standards, the demands of that culture started out reasonable. For James I's Banqueting Hall, in central London (to replace the hall in which *The Tempest* was first performed) a thousand tonnes of freestone were required. For St Paul's, begun fifty years later, fifty further years were required to build it and fifty thousand tonnes of stone. The world is still admiring the result. One of the west towers was designed to house a giant telescope while the cathedral was under construction.

Two hundred years on, Victorian convicts cut and lifted five million tonnes for Portland Harbour's breakwater. From tea rooms nearby a better class of person could watch them work. They built what was then the largest artificial harbour in the world, for what was then the largest navy in the world. Convicts built the Verne, too, the prison which still overlooks that harbour. The Navy left in 1999 and the prison is now the United Kingdom's second largest Immigration Return Centre. Its current inmates are kept in cells which look out onto walls and barbed wire.

I still visit Portland often and was there again only recently. Perhaps the more significant part of anyone's twenties is passed in sheer bafflement: I still find the island a useful place to put my troubles in some perspective. Take a close interest in any place over time and it will slowly begin to furnish you with answers. Though the answers, when they come, may well take the form of further questions.

The writers who brought me further news, that winter, about how little I knew, were sometimes bleak to the point of debilitating. On the face of things such a disturbed landscape might reinforce this outlook. But after all the National Gallery and the headquarters of the UN are also built of this stuff. How bereft of a language are we? Are we really unable to see the moral distinction between a phoney bungalow with a Doomsday machine in the basement and a St Paul's Cathedral built to double as an observatory? Nothing to choose between an Immigration Return Centre built by convicts and the UN? What this island has given us is not just an excellent product in search of a market, or a scene of desolation, but a language and different ways to speak it, some more truthful than others.

My most recent visit to Portland is relevant in a way. In summer, you can swim off the rocky ledges along its south-eastern edge and that is what the owners of the nearby beach huts like to do. Recently they were notified by a formal letter that a permission granted in 1951 to quarry this part of the island was still active. A meeting was immediately called in a village hall and a group was formed to fight for this coastal strip.

The landscape under threat lines the approach road to the Bill, at Portland's southernmost tip. Hundreds of thousands of people travel that road each year. What they arrive at, after the war zone of the island's top end, is a bird observatory and its garden set in a landscape of fields with some beach huts.

It's true that London, Coventry, Southampton and Exeter were all rebuilt after the war using Portland stone. But more than sixty years on from that original permission, the proposal to clear up on this farthest extremity of the island feels different. I asked a couple of locals from the protest group if there were any misgivings at the time about the quantity of stone removed during the 1950s and 1960s. 'Nobody worried about things running out in those days.'

No. Maybe such scenery felt dispensable in 1950. That it no longer does is telling us something. But what? Or how do we answer those larger questions in the language of this particular place, this particular argument?

We might start by recalling earlier occasions on which our cities have had favours to ask of this long-suffering landscape. We might recall that Robert Hooke, as surveyor after the Great Fire, was appointed to check the stone arriving in London for the city's reconstruction. Hooke was a new kind of explorer, and in his line one of the greatest. He never left the country but performed instead prodigious feats of noticing what was there and always had been. He noticed cell structure in plants. He noticed that about 20 per cent of air seemed to be made of something combustible, though it was not yet called oxygen.

He noticed the ammonites arriving in stone shipped from Portland. They were so large and so unlike any living creatures, that they must, he thought, be the remains of a species 'totally destroyed and annihilated'. Two centuries before Darwin, in other words, Hooke deduced from Portland stone that species are not permanent.

Hooke was an astronomer, too. His Monument to the Great Fire of London was designed to be a giant telescope and the Greenwich Observatory was also his work. We are surely justified in arguing that, both through the amazing inferences he drew from its fossils and the effects he achieved with it as a building material, Hooke's use of Portland stone was, in the deepest sense, both reasoned and imaginative.

And what of our own use of this resource? Are we for uprooting every last corner of this landscape, because a post-war permission says we can? Can we still put this island and its stone to reasoned and imaginative use, or is it too late for that?

It isn't too late. The Mass Extinction Monitoring Observatory (MEMO), scheduled for construction at the top of the island's West Cliff, obtained planning permission and has an architect's design. It was designed as a tribute to what Hooke so precociously noticed. Its sombre, spiralling form, modelled on that of a locally abundant fossil, would comprise an inclined walkway, lined with sculptures, wrapped around a giant central exhibition space or auditorium.

Visitors would learn here to situate humankind in the longer story of life's emergence on this planet. They would leave with a deepened sense of our collective responsibility for the rate at which species and habitats are now disappearing. They would be encouraged to search for ways of developing beyond our past destructiveness, towards each other and the planet. MEMO, in short, would advocate just the kind of new planetary awareness we need. It would be the realisation of what dissidents east and west once called for separately and must now insist upon everywhere.

Theodor Adorno once analysed the press coverage of a dinosaur fossil's discovery in Utah. He speculated that our fascination with dinosaurs was not at all the harmless entertainment it is marketed as, on Dorset's Jurassic Coast or anywhere else. Their true but unconscious meaning for us, he argued, was a 'collective projection' of the monstrous forces at work in the present world. People were using films and news stories about dinosaurs, he thought, to prepare themselves and their children, through these 'gigantic images', for the terrors of our own world. But he saw something else too being expressed in the way we recreate these long-extinct animals. 'The desire for the presence of the most ancient is a hope that animal creation might survive the wrong that man has done it, if not man himself, and give rise to a better species, one that finally makes a success of life,' he wrote.

Jan Patočka's answer to the ever expanding 'front' on which he saw humanity fighting was what he called 'the solidarity of the shaken.' The solidarity he had in mind would emerge in improvised groupings of those who are able to see how nature, both our own and the earth's, is being aggressed by the current order. Whether that's in the current rate of extinctions around the world or in a 1951 permission to quarry along Portland's southern edge. Such fellowships would oppose that order not as some national or doctrinaire formation. They would arise rather from something much more elusive, to register their collective response.

Such a response demands, now, a fundamental re-telling of the core stories about who we are. Patočka once took as his theme Europe's expansion through 'the voyages of discovery and the scramble for control of the earth's riches.' These voyages, he argued, had 'led to the emergence of a completely new form of rea-son, by now the only kind we have. This is a rationalism which, in aiming at mastery over material goods, is in-stead mastered by them, through the search for profit.'

We are all of us, whether we know it or not, the uneasy heirs of that critical moment in human devel-opment. Only a new way of seeing that moment can finally make some benign sense of the global aware-ness it afforded us.

NIGHT FALLS, QUICKLY

The travel narratives of the early explorers are rid-dled with memory-holes and evasions: dates that don't agree, glaring omissions, the merest glimpses of what we should now like to know so much more about. I'm drawn to these muddles that get hushed up and played down and rubbed out. What did those islanders in

Cornwall, or the Eskimos on the other side, make of Davis mapping their world? Drake might be in favour of the dignity of all human beings by the time he and Diego met, but he had commanded slave ships only a few years earlier. Even if Diego was paid the same as European crew-members, how did he fit in socially? What did he think of the West Country or London once he got there? What did they think of him?

Gappiness of this kind is as endemic to historical as to personal memory. The voyage on which Diego eventually died, namely Drake's circumnavigation of 1577–80, is as gappy as any of them. It isn't only 'operational details' that the chroniclers kept so close to their chests. There was, for example, a traumatic episode where the thinness of detail strongly suggests more than the protection of technical data.

Thomas Doughty's execution at Port St Julian is an enduring riddle. There are whole online forums devoted to the subject. I'll summarise briefly. Doughty was a lawyer by training, one of the 'gentleman adventurers' on board. An investor in the voyage, he seems also to have had inside knowledge of its purposes and was made commander of a Portuguese prize taken off the Cape Verde Islands. A chest on board was broken open without the General's authorisation and looted. Amidst the accusations and counter-accusations, Doughty claimed magical powers and sounded out some of his crew as allies in a plot to seize command of the expedition.

The whole affair is very obscure and Doughty's motives are baffling. Class conflict, clash of temperament, political and/or sexual intrigue have all been suggested. The argument had simmered for months by the time they reached Port St Julian, in what is now Argentina. Drake formally charged him as a sorcerer and a traitor, and with attempts at 'hindrance and overthrow' of the voyage. After a trial of dubious legality, Doughty was beheaded.

Every detail of every narrative has been exhaustively picked over. Two centuries later, Dr Johnson confessed himself mystified and two centuries on from Dr Johnson nobody is any the wiser. But another episode, similarly opaque, has received much less attention. It obviously mattered at least as much to those who were there. It is the only event, from the Indonesian section of the journey, on which all accounts are agreed about the date.

After calling at one of the Spice Islands, the *Golden Hinde* had already for some weeks been trying to reach the Indian Ocean. The ship needed to travel west but the prevailing wind and the lie of the land forced it to travel south instead, along rugged coasts and now through uncharted waters off Celebes. Through a maze of islands, deep bays and narrow peninsulas the ship had laboriously picked its way until, on the evening of 9 January 1580, open water at last appeared up ahead. It must have been a huge relief to everybody.

The crew, half way round the world and more

than two years out of Plymouth, knew they were now approaching the start of the long run homewards. Ballasted with treasure, additionally loaded with six tonnes of spices, the vessel's hull was low in the water but freshly careened and this was a state-of-the-art war ship. Fortune had been with them. The General ordered full sail to be set.

We know a curious fact about Drake's daily routine. He retired to his cabin promptly at eight, every evening, presumably to complete the day's entry in that long-since-vanished log book. Yet this fact is never placed alongside another: when the *Golden Hinde* struck a reef that evening, it was at 'the beginning of the first watch', which is to say, just after eight o'clock.

In an over-confident novice it would have been a disastrous blunder. In a mariner of Drake's standing, it was something stranger and far worse. His authority rested upon his abilities as a navigator and a man of action. The strangely sloping weather deck, as the crew swarmed up on to it, and the realisation that their General was capable of such an error, must have seemed unbelievable at first, then deeply disorienting.

That order to set full sail, at nightfall, upon a sea for which they had no reliable charts, was one of the very rare occasions on which this great navigator spectacularly misjudged his situation. A short time after the order was given, the vessel lurched abruptly to starboard and rose out of the water, stuck fast, keeling over dangerously. The same strong wind that had so recently filled its sails with fresh hope, now jammed its timbers against this 'shoal' and held them there. It was now all that prevented the ship's rolling off and capsizing at once.

This was the 16th century's Apollo 13 moment. Night had just fallen, quickly, as it does in the Tropics. They had no reliable charts and the nearest land was about twenty miles away. Mission Control, for these stranded sons of Renaissance Europe, was still somewhere like Heaven, not somewhere like Houston.

The wind holding them fast kept up for twenty hours. The episode is generally treated as a frightening but mercifully brief interruption to the *Golden Hinde*'s progress around the planet and into the history books. That is certainly a view which the officially sanctioned accounts encourage. But in the first of those versions, published nine years after their return, the entire episode is glossed over in one and a half paragraphs. This reticence will have been no accident. Those involved were still alive, with interests to safeguard. Almost half a century must pass before *The World Encompassed*, the first full official account, would appear. Though more detail is given there, striking contradictions and omissions remain.

There exists also the curiously fragmented 'Anonymous Memorandum', which casts doubt on both of these accounts. This Memorandum has long been well known to historians and its authenticity is not in question, but it includes two phrases which have not, to my knowledge, been much dwelt upon.

The ship, of course, survived the ordeal. Had it turned out otherwise the History Channel would be searching still for The Lost Treasure of Pelican. Once the ship had regained the open sea, Drake summoned the ship's chaplain, Francis Fletcher, and ordered him to be shackled to a 'staple' driven into the forecastle deck. We have already encountered Fletcher the wildlife watcher. Not long out of Cambridge when he joined the expedition, he had meanwhile travelled in Italy and as we'll see he appears to have acted on board as a physician as well as the crew's confessor. Protestant opinion took hygienic reform of conditions on English ships seriously, which can only have enhanced Fletcher's status. A Spanish prisoner noted that he was highly respected by the crew, who listened attentively to his sermons.

The notes he made about this section of the voyage were long ago lost. But what the Anonymous Memorandum tells us is that, shortly after this narrow escape, Drake 'ex-communicated' Fletcher 'out of the Church of God, and from all the benefits and graces thereof.' He called him 'the falsest knave that liveth' and furthermore 'denounced' him 'to the devil and all his angels.'

Clearly there had been a disagreement. From the official narrative we gather that there were, broadly speaking, three things which happened during the stranding. Fletcher did the religion: he preached, led prayers and finally, when all hope was lost, he offered communion. Drake took on the technical side, descending into the hold to man the bilge pump. The ship was found not to be taking on much water, so he waited for daylight then took the boat out to look for any ground within 300 fathoms to which they could fasten the anchor, thereby levering the ship off the rock. Finally, it is known that the crew threw several cannons and three tonnes of spices over the side, before the wind shifted and the ship was re-floated.

It has always been assumed that Fletcher, as he preached, interpreted their stranding as divine retribution, particularly for Doughty's execution. That seems very likely but Drake's words hint at more than that. Those who knew Drake described him as a well-spoken man. The violence of these words suggests that he has just had a very nasty fright.

It must have been through his chaplain's preaching that the offence had come, so the theological inflection to Drake's insults, denouncing Fletcher 'to the devil and all his angels', will have been no accident. Angels, in January 1580, were no sentimental frippery and the devil certainly wasn't. These years take far more of their colouring from the Middle Ages than we are accustomed to imagine. The existence of angels was still believed in quite literally and the devil also had command of several squadrons. His had fallen through pride, through turning their minds away from

God and his creation, to admire their own 'sublimity and honour' instead. They were to be found scattered throughout the physical universe, hiding in caves and mines, for example, from which they emerged to do men harm.

Even stranger is the other phrase that has been missed. Drake threatened to hang him if he ever again even once came 'before the mast'. That last phrase refers to the part of the ship where the crew lived. This is clearly an accusation that Fletcher had tried to incite a mutiny. It also strongly suggests he had met with some success. 'The General', in other words, had found his authority seriously questioned during those twenty hours and Fletcher had done the questioning. This was about much more than the dubious legality of Doughty's execution. Questions about Drake's leadership and the expedition's purpose had been opened up at a critical moment and by a highly-respected member of the crew.

We are not told exactly what those questions were, but we can make a pretty good guess. We can certainly do better than explain them away as some kind of left-over from the Doughty Affair, but the trial at Port St Julian offers some useful hints. During and after the trial, Drake made two related but contradictory points about class. He argued in a speech to the jury that the voyage could not continue with Doughty alive and promised rewards unlike any they had known. If they sailed on 'the worst in this fleet shall become a gentleman.' In context, this was not far short of a bribe. Drake was offering them a share in the treasure and a leg up the social ladder. But at a religious service after the beheading, he interrupted Fletcher to deliver a 'sermon' himself, threatening anyone who questioned his command from now on with the same fate. Doughty's treachery was traceable to the idleness of his class, he argued now. The 'gentlemen' and the 'mariners' were now to 'hale and draw together.'

He offered his crew, in other words, a new start, a personal interest in the plunder and a deceased hate figure, in the form of Doughty, who was alleged to have conspired against their bettering themselves in this way. So when Fletcher raised the question of their later shipwreck as divine retribution, it would have been retribution not only for Doughty's execution but for the crew's complicity in that death. In re-opening the question he went right to the heart of what the voyage had been for.

LISTENING WITH AN EARTHENWARE POT

Francis Fletcher was an educated man who had, for more than two years now, heard the confessions and tended the injuries of crew-members. He had won their confidence. These were men who had enlisted for a trading voyage to Egypt. They had not enlisted for a three year journey to the ends of the earth. There are clear signs that on this, as on other long-range voyages of the time, what we would call depression was a problem. But he knew also that to weigh freedom from all debt, forever, to weigh long coveted fields and houses, not to mention bragging rights, against abstractions like justice, is to ask much.

Francis Drake had received little formal education and was keenly conscious of this. He was, however, one of the world's great navigators and a famous man. He also knew his crew, but as their General and, ultimately, as their paymaster. His authority rested on the ability to bring his men home and make them rich. His skills as a man of action would make this possible.

There is another curious circumstance here which historians do not dwell on. All detailed accounts are agreed that the cannon were jettisoned only after Fletcher had preached and celebrated communion. By then, almost an entire day had passed since the ship ran aground. Drake's hesitation is of course understandable: he was loath to disarm the vessel. He was by then the most wanted man on the planet. Indeed, we know, as he could only guess, that the flotilla of Spanish ships sent to intercept him left harbour in the very same week that the *Golden Hinde* was 'delayed' off Celebes. The ship was still only half way around the world: to complete this journey un-armed would be a gigantic risk. Drake had only just blundered as never before and had now, additionally, to explain to his men that he was not going to lighten the vessel by the readiest means available.

Fletcher could do little more, at first, than seek to contain some of the hysteria. He would have done so in the language of the time. Doubt not, he would have assured them, that from death we go straight into life. He would have meant it, too. This was an age of literal faith and he was that faith's official representative on board. A lamp unto our feet and a light unto our path is God's word. He would have called upon the Judge of all men, in all ages, in all places, to visit them here with His spirit.

Of your great goodness, merciful father, you have fashioned us even of the dust to be living creatures according to your image. Your providence has breathed into us also the knowledge of our salvation in the redemption of Christ. Visit us now on these horrible seas and fearful waves – visit us in the greatness of your fatherly kindness and fortify our faith that we waver not in this most perilous place and dangerous time.

Once these negotiations with the celestial powers were underway, Tom Moone would have been sent below decks. Moone was a large man, a hedonistic and violent mercenary and a firm friend of the General's. He had personally guarded Thomas Doughty as he awaited 'trial' and seems to have taken keen pleasure in terrorising and robbing the Spanish inhabitants of coastal settlements. As ship's carpenter on one of

Drake's earlier expeditions, he had been trusted to carry out secret orders to scuttle a vessel. Someone was needed now who could remove decking at speed, allowing access to the damaged timbers. Moone had the skill, the physical courage and the devotion to Drake. He would surely have made one of the small party which made that descent.

Fletcher would have noted Tom Moone and other of the General's 'old heavy friends' being sent below. As Fletcher prayed on deck, these men fetched from the galley an earthenware pot to detect the exact location of any broken timbers. Placed with its open end against the lower deck, an ear pressed against its base would detect a low roaring when they had found the place.

Was it the absence of Drake's closest allies or the urgency of their plight or both which inspired Fletcher to venture certain risky suggestions? The scriptures and the Church Fathers are, after all, not exactly silent about this kind of thing.

He that loveth gold shall not be justified, and he that followeth corruption shall have enough thereof. Gold hath been the ruin of many, and their destruction was present. It is a stumbling-block unto them that sacrifice unto it, and every fool shall be taken therewith.

Fletcher would certainly have been able to summon such verses.

Or did he venture even closer to the bone? *And men go forth to admire lofty mountains and the ocean and the course of the stars, and forget their own selves while doing so.* Knowing passages of St Augustine would have been one way to taunt the General. Would he have refrained now, when Drake, who gave no quarter himself, had never looked so vulnerable?

Or was it, rather, as much as Fletcher could do to hold their attention at all as the vessel shifted uneasily beneath them, bumping against the reef, ready to split at any moment? Might it have been in silence rather that they prayed?

From that part of his notes which has survived, it's clear he interpreted the ship's treatment by the elements as a direct and literal expression of God's verdict on their behaviour. Of a fifty-six-day storm which the ship had survived in the South Pacific, he wrote:

it Pleased him againe for his name sake to heare the prayers of them wch vnfeignedly called vpon his holly & reuerend name . . . Wherefore hee caused the Sonn by day & the moon & stars by night to shine vpon vs.

There is no reason to imagine he saw this present disaster any differently. Indeed, that it had struck precisely when the ship was farthest from home would surely have impressed him as significant. God had given them exactly half the circumference of the globe to reveal to Him their true purpose in setting out.

The assumption that a technical competence would see them through had been abruptly suspended. This switch back to a religious interpretation of the voyage was accompanied by a sudden inversion of the command structure. And both of these, for Fletcher, were part of a divine plan to rescue this mission from itself.

This was dangerous reasoning but as an experienced preacher, he could quickly have sought refuge in generalisation.

Thou most dear father who hast alone the ends of all things in thy hands, watch over thy servants with thy holy power. May the frailty of our flesh never drive us into doubt of your loving kindness. That were death indeed, but they only need fear death that are troubled in their consciences and seek not your comfort.

But this surely was the time to speak truly. Now or not at all. He might well have raised, perhaps obliquely, the subject of Doughty, might have expressed his regret at having not done more to save him, at having gone along, however grudgingly, with Drake's 'deal'. Now was the time to attend to that deeper self-inflicted moral injury from which they were all suffering. The Doughty he recalled to the men then, or re-invented for the occasion, would have been invested with many fine qualities. He would have been the man who had questioned Drake's plans from the outset. The man who had seen that their future swoop on the Spanish trading routes would be actuated by greed. That it would, at the same moment, both succeed brilliantly and ruin them morally. So here it all was, come horribly true.

Drake observed this brinkmanship closely. With the crew in their present mood, he wanted most of them where he could see them. Tom Moore now re-appeared, briefly conferred with Drake, then again went below. Fletcher faltered at the sight of him, the crew too were distracted, and Drake seized the initiative. Drake often led services himself. This was no time, and it would not have been in character, even in this most precarious moment of his career, to allow such a sermon to continue. He interrupted with some words of his own. Their tone was that of the bluff commander – I imagine them a little self-consciously jaunty, to disguise both the injury and the shame.

To preach the Gospel with no fine rhetoric, Master Fletcher, lest the Cross of Our Redeemer should lose its power to speak home – such is the Minister's true office. A Minister does not give up his ship for lost, any more than he may give up a soul for lost. Matters regarding the ship fall rather within the Captain's competency. Of souls, too, I may perhaps speak, when the chaplain is so eager to fear the worst. I am content – so may we all be – that my soul goes hence to a far better place, when God wills it. For his part, furthermore, the Captain fears there has been some sharp altercation between our ship and a certain Signor Rock. What think you, Master Parson? Shall we endeavour to part them or no?

That he personally went below to man the bilge pumps is usually cited as evidence of a great captain in action. He left the mere Fletchers of this world to moralise their dilemma into a thousand similes. But it is also possible that the Drake who sought in this way to divert attention back to his competency in practical matters was a dangerously isolated commander, scrambling to reassert his badly damaged authority. And simultaneously fleeing and terminating a sermon he wanted no more of.

The bilge water would also, it's worth mentioning, have been the best guide to the state of the hull. What he would have feared, as the first bucket filled, was sea water that smelt just like sea water. Bilge water in a sealed hull soon develops its own unmistakable reek, especially in the Tropics. Drake manned the pumps himself because he wanted to be the first to know what the bilge smelt like. It smelt bad, which was great news. The hull was still sound. The *Golden Hinde* was not finished yet, and neither was he.

We should imagine the crew meanwhile waiting up on deck for the sound of a bell. For even here Drake had managed to work in a No-Popery feature: Spanish prisoners who were shown around the vessel reported their indignation at seeing a bell looted from a church set up above the bilge pump. If Drake needed help, he would have rung that bell. He didn't ring it. A little credibility had been salvaged.

As day broke, the tide had still not floated them

clear. The ship's boat was lowered. If lead and line could detect good ground anywhere close by, the ship's anchor would be fastened upon the sea bed, creating a fixed point by which the ship could be prised loose from the rocky cleft in which she had stuck fast.

THE BARBAROUS PEOPLE OF THE HEATHEN

Time and again the crew would have seen the lead drop and then watched as the line was paid out after it. The sloping deck offered a clear view of these proceedings to anyone who could bear to watch. Three hundred fathoms of line found nothing all morning and faith in the General's abilities continued to ebb away. As they had prayed for a high tide to lift them off, now they prayed for the low tide to bring some sea bed within reach. But the tide here, it seemed, was no Christian tide. The wind which neither slackened nor strengthened held them upright here, but was that wind an agent of the Christian God, or was it rather the agent of some foreign demon? The longer this lasted, the greater the strain upon the ship's structure and their exhausted nerves alike.

The swift and violent end for which they had first prepared themselves gave way now, in their sleep-deprived ruminations, to an even grislier scenario. It lurked just below the everyday consciousness of any long-distance mariner in that age. The ship was built to last, after all. She might remain here, intact, for weeks, while they quickly ran through their supplies. Perhaps God had devised a more cunning set of torments.

It is significant that, in the narrative we have, the sailors speculate at this point about the 'barbarous people of the heathen' which are sure to inhabit that island looming on the horizon. It is, of course, a property of the barbarous people of the heathen that they eat not only each other but also and especially any strangers that chance upon their shore. It was surely the prospect of cannibalism – their own – which they were actually contemplating.

We should consider also that they were two degrees south of the equator in the hottest season of the year. Strong winds might have taken the edge off the worst of the heat and humidity but would only have added to the dangers of dehydration. The ship's boat carried twenty at most. They were fifty-nine. Which twenty would sail with the General if he decided to leave?

Any departure was sure to be justified as a search for fresh water. Those who wished to believe that were free to do so. Meanwhile the thirst intensified and the water they had was strictly rationed. As they watched that vain search for some sea-bed, even as they prayed, they must also have been remembering, doing the calculation in their heads. Would it be those who had spoken up for Doughty, or those who had kept quiet? Is it not highly likely that Drake set an armed guard on the weapons store the moment his ship hit?

None of this is to suggest that the chaplain and the crew did not continually implore the Heavens to be merciful as they watched from that tilted deck. *God does not delight in the death of a sinner.* It was not to be believed that the reef could fall away beneath them so steeply on all sides. Christ would be merciful yet.

The image of these men as maritime heroes and/or international gangsters is so deeply imprinted that the scene on that deck, as the last hope trickled away, is hard for us to picture. Their famous General, out there on the water, the day after his nightmare mistake, would not, I think, have resembled very closely that Son of Devon who smiled confidently from the pages of *Proud Heritage*. Haggard, sleepless, here was a man in serious trouble. Tossed violently back and forth in a little boat on an angry sea, he desperately cast about for the luck which had abruptly deserted him.

Having taken that boat as close to the reef as he dared, Drake gives the order to return to the ship. As he steps on board, having found nothing, so those other explanations for the disaster, hinted at earlier by the chaplain, surge back to the fore. One source records that Drake walked with a slight limp, from a gun-shot wound sustained years earlier. If it had once seemed to lend him a martial swagger, to enhance his legendary aura, it only added now to the air of dejection as he rejoined his crew. The ingenuity of the greatest mariner on the planet cannot avail against the truth: their collision with this rock is divine retribution.

Drake knows this is the perception he is returning to. He has put it off for as long as he can. But at last his wizardry has failed him and failed them all. The ship's boat is swung back onto the weather deck and secured against the railings. It is 'by general voice determined' that the chaplain shall give a sermon and then offer communion.

EARTH, ASHES AND EMERALDS

Francis Fletcher left Plymouth with a physician's chest in his cabin, but less than six months into the voyage the bottles of medicine inside were all smashed during a storm off Brazil. By the time they made landfall on the other side of the Atlantic he had nothing to treat the crew, many of whom were ill. He found that seal fat would heal sores, 'whereof diuers of our men had good Experience by my directions to their great comfortes.' He went in search of medicinal herbs, too. The expedition lost its surgeon early on and Fletcher's notes suggest that he filled the vacant role. It is worth noting that it was a pharmacist who later took such care to copy out his narrative.

His physician's chest somehow came to the attention of the Patagonian Indians with whom they made contact in the (southern) winter of 1578. Fletcher seems to have liked them. His warm account of their hospitality and egalitarian society immediately precedes his account of Doughty's show trial and execution and the implied contrast is hard to miss. The use they made of plants and animal fats interests him too and he is attracted by their love of music. They, in turn, discover hitherto unsuspected potential in his physician's chest full of broken bottles. Much to its owner's delight, they put it to use as a novelty percussion instrument.

When Drake threatened Doughty's supporters after the execution, the chaplain would have been among those he was addressing. Yet only weeks later, having broken through into the Pacific, Drake was hit in the face with an arrow during a fight with indigenous people on the island of Mocha. Might it not have been Fletcher who extracted the tip and tended the wound? Fletcher would certainly have prayed with Diego, Drake's servant, as he died from wounds received in the same fight. Did this restore the bond of trust, or only put it under further strain?

Perhaps they hardly knew themselves. Less than two weeks later, after the attack on Santiago de Chile, Drake gave gold fittings taken from the cathedral there to Fletcher. Was this as close as the great man came to apologising? Was it thanks? But in England, Catholicism at this time was closely associated with the witchcraft of which Doughty had been accused. Was this an insult, then, or barbed with mockery, an accusation of some hidden weakness for Popery? Or was he deliberately aiming at a sinister incoherence? In any case, Drake was known to them all, but especially to

Fletcher, as a man of flesh and blood, as vulnerable to injury and, it now appeared, as liable to error as anyone else.

The Fletcher, then, who addressed the crew on that deck more than a year later, addressed men he knew well at the very limits of their endurance. This was the experienced crew of a state-of-the-art war ship, utterly undone by a single calamitous error of judgement. This voyage had transformed their expectations so many times already, but the future had never been so dark. He had more than a license to say exactly what he thought. He had a duty to do so. One subject in particular would have been fresh in his mind.

Maria was one of three or four slaves they had taken during their run up the western sea board of the Americas. If that really was her name, was she Catholic, then, when they found her? Did the crew of the *Golden Hinde* proceed to impress upon her the virtues of the Protestant faith? Was she convinced? She was pregnant, anyway, by the time the ship reached the Spice Islands. Drake left her and the two other black passengers on the island where they had spent some time careening the ship and feasting on crayfish so enormous that one of them could feed three or four men.

Another anonymous account, the 'Short Abstract of the Present Voyage', written by a crew-member, states that Maria became pregnant 'between the captaine and his men pirats.' It is quite possible that this reflects nothing but somebody's intense dislike of the General. But even William Camden, a contemporary and an admirer, reproached his conduct in this affair. The 'fair Negroess' had been 'given him for a present by a Spaniard whose Ship he had spared.' His conduct in setting her 'on Shoar' had been 'inhumane'.

The 'falsest knave that liveth': that is how Drake damns his chaplain. This can only be the response to a very serious accusation. Since none of the official accounts tells us what it was, what are the other possibilities?

There was da Silva, too. The Portuguese pilot, seized along with his ship off the Cape Verde Islands, was pressed into service as their guide to the Brazil coast. He seems to have been popular. Both Drake and Fletcher befriended him. He also attended their religious services and was seen doing so by Spanish prisoners, who were sure to report that to the Inquisition once they were set free. So to abandon da Silva to his fate in Guatalco, Mexico, the following year was certainly to abandon him to the ministrations of the Holy Office.

Seen a certain way, Drake might stand accused of many things. Daring master of surprises, he caught the Spanish napping: isn't that how the story runs? But Fletcher could have turned that against him easily enough. They had been taken for Spaniards or Portuguese everywhere they went in the Pacific, because no English boat had ever been seen there before. Like the Spanish and the Portuguese, they wore beards, too.

Their equipment and their appearance were barely distinguishable from those of their enemies. Yes, that had given them a tactical edge. But what if their motives, too, were identical to those of their enemies? Had English greed not proved to be much the same as Spanish greed?

These would have been dangerous arguments, coming from a chaplain of all people. But some such 'dangerous argument' certainly was raised. Wasn't their cover, about a new religion through which Christ would set the world free, really just that, a cover? Protestant fig-leaf trumps Catholic one. To question this would have come perilously close to treason. But perhaps this is where the reference to the devil and all his angels comes from. What if this new gloves-off Fletcher represented the *gould* and *sylver* in their hold as devils? Their condemnation of Doughty, their seizure of one ship after another since – these had been forms of devil worship. Here, now, was the destruction they had brought upon themselves.

No 300 fathoms of line would ever come close to measuring the depth of the trouble they were in. He would have argued, with St Paul, that the wisdom of this world is foolishness before God.

You who have knowledge of our innermost hearts, keep us from all sinful intentions and injurious dealings with our fellow men. Grant that we may possess at last the heavenly wisdom to do as we ought.'

For the Greeks, as Fletcher would have known well, eyesight was a divine gift allowing men to admire and study the heavens. This was how they had learnt to harmonise the natural truth of reason within them and the divine reason which governed the stars in their courses. This was how they learnt to regulate their actions. But what the General had applied to the heavens instead was the wisdom of this world. Their skills, their compasses and quadrants and traverse boards, had warped their understanding all down one side. They might think of themselves as the new men but theirs was merely the old sin of pride.

An illustration would have come to mind easily enough. The two brightest stars in the Little Bear, known as 'the Guards' for their proximity to the Pole Star, were used by mariners as a clock and would certainly have been used so by the crew of the *Golden Hinde*, just as the Southern Cross was, and is, used in the southern hemisphere. Were the heavens, then, a time-piece, a useful appliance, an ingenious device? Was this what the new learning amounted to? Had it made of the stars so many navigational aids, so many pegs by which to lever ourselves back and forth about the world?

But *seek her early*, said the Preacher, *wisdom is worth more than emeralds. Neither breadth nor space shall keep us from the Word of God*, said Paul.

If you, Lord, have determined to gather us to your people, so prepare us every one that our death may be to your glory and to the salvation of our souls. We are but earth and ashes. Possess us at last, oh Lord, with a holy unity, in the fear and love of your majesty . . .

In what they all took to be their last moments upon earth, what flashed upon the preacher's inner eye was all they *might* have sailed for, and had not. He implored these men to send each one of them a fathom line deep into his own heart, to sound his own motives and actions, right to the bottom, to see them for what they had been and repent at last, while a little time was still left to move God's pity.

But this was not yet his final word. He had listened the previous day, with the rest of the crew, to Drake's order that the guns were not to be thrown over the side. In God's name he now countermanded that order, adding that as much of the cargo as was ready to hand should also be jettisoned. And he added a proviso, a saving clause, the crucial distinction that made this an act of obedience, all be it to a higher authority. This action, he argued, would only find favour with God if every man, in carrying it out, acknowledged his part in the collective guilt and in this way unburdened himself of it. It must be their souls and not their ship only which they sought to lighten.

So Fletcher preached. The import of his words would not have been lost upon his listeners as he prepared the sacraments and invited the crew of the *Golden Hinde* to the Lord's table. It was a dangerous

Christ they remembered that day on the sloping deck. And moments later, in bundling those sacks of ginger and cloves and pimento through the main deck gun ports, each one worth its weight in silver, the longing for redemption and survival were completely fused. To the General this was mutiny, but Fletcher had claimed to be speaking on God's orders and Drake would have been a fool to contradict him. His command was, in effect, suspended.

Perhaps the behaviour of the crew just as the wind began to swing round would have been most mysterious of all. They would have been attuned, for twenty hours, to the slightest change in its direction or force. Perhaps even below deck they were so at one with this vessel by now, they would have sensed the alteration in a moment. There was nothing of theology in this. This was mastery of a craft pure and simple. And the moment this change was detected, the polarity of the situation was instantly reversed once again.

THE FIRST SIGNATURE

Tom Brewer was Drake's trumpeter and definitely one of the General's 'old heavy friends'. But I like to think at this moment at least, he came into his own. Drake in the same moment recovered all his daring. Just as it had been lost, so his whole reputation was restored to him now, in an instant. *There came a bearing Gale of wind on one Side, as if it were sent from Heaven.*

By some channel of communication unknown even to themselves, the crew took to their stations at once. This would be a matter of split-second timing. But he was the man to carry this off if anyone was. With the first change in the wind the ship seemed only to settle back a little further on her timbers. True, the ship was now lighter and responded more readily than it might have, but what Drake gathered from that slight movement was that this was none other than the extraordinary hand of God reaching down to them.

The signal Brewer gave was unlike any blast on that trumpet he had ever given: to more than one sailor, dangling aloft, frantically unfurling sail, at the limits of exhaustion, heads swimming with religious imagery and fear and remorse, it must have seemed like Judgement Day. The ship began a roll from which it could not possibly recover. Nothing could prevent them now from going the same way as their guns and merchandise. You could almost feel the water reaching in through those empty gun ports to pull the ship under. They clung on – what else was there? – as the ship heeled and rolled, then bucked and kicked.

The *Golden Hinde* sat gently righting herself alongside the reef, water streaming from her decks, risen from the waves to new life. But the General remained all vigilance, his eyes on the rapidly filling sails now easing the ship away from what it had been pinned against. They appeared to be free of all obstruction but must not lurch, now, into further trouble. He instructed the steersman, called on mariners above to reduce sail, ordered any remaining unspoilt cargo to be returned to the hold. The *Golden Hinde* was Francis Drake's ship once again. He set a special watch as the ship, more cautiously this time, threaded her way south. Brewer's trumpet was heard again, calling gentlemen and crew to a general assembly in the forecastle.

Fletcher, wherever Drake's 'heavy friends' found him out, would have been 'brought thither like a prisoner', just as Doughty had been before his trial. Drake probably knew that to execute him outright would make a mutiny more likely rather than less. But he wanted to give Fletcher the fright of his life and let everyone watch, lest anyone be tempted ever again to see in him an alternative commander.

Drake addressed the prisoner sitting on a chest – I picture him cross-legged, in a kind of celebrity-yogic posture, his informal, CEO manner fairly crackling with a fiendish mischief. As in the appeal he had made during Doughty's trial, he would have taken this earliest opportunity to remind everybody just how rich they would soon be, if they only trusted in him now.

I fasten this posy that I have composed, thus, about the prisoner's arm and assure you all, before I answer Master Fletcher's sermon, of one last thing. I make a solemn promise. By God's mercy, we shall reach England again. The King of Spain, through his envoys at court, shall surely petition the

Queen upon our return. Just as he did when we, chancing upon certain overloaded mules in the hills above Nombre de Dios, gently relieved them of their intolerable burden. Once again the Spaniard will urge that we restore to them what they have lost through their own negligence.

And we, my friends, shall swear in writing that the sums of which they speak are much exaggerated. So we shall. Only silver and some gold was here and there taken – how much we know not. But a very small sum in relation to what is reported. So we shall swear, every one of us. And among the signatures to that deposition, Francis Fletcher, yours shall be the first.

It was all very well for the Fletchers of this world, he would have continued, already warm to his theme, all very well for the Francis Fletchers, with their college learning, to talk. His own education had been other-wise. Would Fletcher be so scornful of the world as it was now opening up if his family had paid rents to the abbot and patched cob walls, had eaten cheese and watched the roof beams blacken, one generation after another? He would not so lightly condemn the new freedom, with all its risks, if he had known the old incarceration, and its wretchedness.

Might he not have reminded them of how he him-self had watched the King's men carrying away their old landlord's treasure, from Tavistock Abbey, tak-ing it away to the Tower of London? Likewise, now, it would take Philip five years to make up the losses they had inflicted on his reserves of silver and gold. It was only thus that the Anti-Christ would be brought to nothing. Did the chaplain really think God had no purpose in placing these means, rather, in the hands of true believers than in those of idolaters and blasphemers? How little did this 'chaplain' trust in his own religion! How poorly did he understand the ways of his own God!

He had claimed their very use of the stars was in breach of God's law, when God himself had created and ordained 'the lights in the firmament of heaven' to be 'for signs and for seasons and for days and for years', for the measurement of time, that is. How then was it against God's will to use them as just that? Why had he accepted the gifts the General offered him, the golden ornaments taken from the church in Santiago de Chile, if he despised riches? And why had he agreed, with everyone else, to sail for a share of the proceeds, if his conscience was against it? If Doughty had been a wronged gentleman, if he was a sacrificial lamb upon the altar of gold and silver, then why had he, Fletcher, signed the deposition against him?

Whatever it was that had stung Drake so in the sermon would certainly have been answered now. To the suggestion that he had abandoned, never mind misused, Maria, he would have given no quarter. Yet I suspect it would have been upon his honour as a Christian that he rejected the suggestion. If there was any truth in the charge that he had 'got rid' of Maria and the child, he might well have answered that Fletcher was fully complicit. He would have had to baptise the child, making him responsible for it. This was why he had not objected to leaving them there.

And was it only with terror of the sentence to be passed that Fletcher listened to this? Was this a trial? Did he feel his own complicity in Maria's abandonment? Or wonder, even for a moment, how it might have been to sail into Plymouth Sound with that child on board?

What they had done was not unlawful, the General continued. It was merely untried. In every age there are those who understand that distinction and those who do not. Those who condemn it as unlawful are, like most of humanity, clinging to the wreckage of the old forms. And there they would perish if those who understood the times better came not to their aid. He knew men well: that was why he had not told them where the ship was really bound. They would live to thank him for it, but they would have to trust and obey him first. It was not only for the silver that they had sailed. Above all, it was the future they had been entrusted to go out and find and fetch home again, in the name of the living God.

Fletcher's sermon he condemned as a shameful loss of self-command, as both an act of insubordination, tending to undermine the Captain's authority, but worse than that, as tending to undermine that general discipline without which no ship ever came home safe. It was true: the gold and silver were what others would admire, on their return. And let there be no canting about this: they won't be wrong to admire it either. But the self-command required to bring it back – this was beyond the comprehension of ordinary men. And yet it was better known to the simplest man on this ship, than to the chaplain himself.

'For your false sermon, delivered with intent to weaken the men's resolve in our time of greatest peril, I do hereby ex-communicate you out of the church of God, and from all the benefits and graces thereof, and I denounce you to the devil and all his angels. I charge you furthermore not once to come before the mast. If you do, I swear I shall see you hanged!'

The crowd parted to allow the General passage. One or two pressed forward immediately to read the verse for themselves, hardly able to believe its wording could truly be as their General said it was. Tom Drake, burly brother and reliable henchman, stood solemnly over the former chaplain, appointed to stand guard and very proud indeed of the appointment. For those too far away to read it for themselves, or disinclined, perhaps, to try, he eagerly lent his assistance: 'Francis Fletcher, the falsest knave that lives!' he cried out, then resumed his grinning, complacent airs.

Some there were that met Tom's eye and some that smiled, too, as they did so, but upon most the effect of the General's angry words was still working. One or two might savour the savagely comic touches of his performance but its larger meaning was now added to the still astonishing fact of their having survived at all. And which among them could fault the General? He had never faltered. He had maintained his good humour even after all hope was seemingly gone and so had been prepared, uncannily so, the moment it returned. He had been vindicated.

And yet there was in this crowing over Fletcher, plainly, also a deep and dangerous insecurity. Drake's harshness reminded many of how fully persuaded they had been by the chaplain's sermon. Not everyone went quite so far as Tom in his admiration for the General.

The crew went their ways with a general uneasiness, knowing this question now officially closed. Each man, as he went, stowed it below decks as best he could, hammering down planks, securing hatches. Though for some days, certain glances exchanged could not but betray them to one another.

It was above all by the looks they did not exchange with Fletcher during the weeks he spent there exposed to general derision, that they communicated, each to himself, that the matter was not closed and never would be. Fletcher in chains and that 'posy' around his arm set the General's seal of ownership upon this story. And it has been in his ownership ever since. Under those planks and hatches this story has lain, for four centuries and more.

The return of the treasure was indeed demanded by the Spanish upon the ship's arrival in England. Elizabeth famously responded by having Drake knighted. Where exactly upon his ship, she asked her favourite sea

captain, would he like to receive the honour? He selected the weather deck, just by the capstan where Fletcher
had preached, so that the assembled dignitaries and the
crew – but most of all so that Francis Fletcher himself –
should have as clear a view as possible.

In private the Queen is said to have quipped she
was so cross with Drake that she would 'take away all
his treasure'. He was actually paid some ten thousand
pounds. A further eight thousand was distributed
to the crew. The rest was paid out to investors. The
quantity of precious metals claimed by the Spanish
authorities was denied by the crew, in writing. The
first signature at the foot of the document, which still
exists, is that of Francis Fletcher.

THE MEDICINAL POWERS OF DRAGON ROOT

To say that everyone is agreed on the date of this near-
miss is not quite accurate. Most sources say the ship
struck on the 9th, one or two say the 8th. On their return to England the crew of the *Golden Hinde* found,
like Magellan's crew at Sanlúcar before them, that
they had lost a day. Their log presumably said they had
struck the reef on the 8th but most sources corrected
the date, retrospectively, to the 9th. The 'International
Date Line' which today runs down the middle of the
Pacific did not then exist. Any ship crossing it now
puts its clock forward by one day.

It may be objected – in fact it surely will be – that to expend, as I just have, such effort on fanciful but ultimately idle speculations is to commit the most elementary of freshman errors. By all means indulge your childish re-enactments, your pantomime, but the only question anyone asked when the *Golden Hinde* got back was: How much loot? And the entire crew evidently swore not to tell. End of.

———

Whilst the *Golden Hinde* was sailing on through the Spice Islands with its chaplain in shackles, Carolus Clusius, in faraway Vienna, was writing his name and the date (11 January 1580) at the end of a long letter to a German prince. He had just made a list of suggestions for the new botanical garden being laid out in Heidelberg. Clusius, as Europe's leading expert on exotic plants and a tireless correspondent with other collectors, was a natural choice as royal advisor. His list has survived. It is twenty-five pages and one hundred and fifty species long.

It's fun finding out about people like Carolus Clusius. I do recommend it. My experience of palaces is limited, but the Bishop's Palace in Exeter is easily the nicest one I've met. Unassuming, situated half-way down the least frequented approach to the cathedral, you can make some of it out from the road, behind several big old trees and lots of holly. Towered over by the cathedral on the north side, it overlooks a walled garden to the south. It is home to a music school as well as the cathedral archive.

Clusius, unlike our TV historians, had more questions about than ready-made answers to Drake's Famous Voyage. He therefore got himself to London, where he was staying with a friend and fellow natural- ist early in 1581. Once there he did what any sensible person would have done. What's really strange is that nobody else thought of it: he talked to Drake and to as many of his crew as he could.

This was altogether in character. Born in Arras, Clusius worked and travelled all over Europe. In fact, he never left it, but quickly saw the implications of the non-European peoples and plants and animals being encountered by the explorers. He later spoke to two Indians in Holland, from Gujarat and Bengal, about the trees and fruits of their native land. He was the first man to scientifically describe the potato. Ditto the penguin. He imported the first tulip into Holland. His cabinet of curiosities in Leiden, and the educational garden he designed and laid out in the same city, were famous throughout Europe.

We are fortunate indeed that such a man secured interviews with Drake and his crew on their return. The result, discreetly published in Antwerp as additional 'notes' on the work of a Spanish botanist, appeared in 1582. The English government having ordered an information black-out, this is the first substantial account of the circumnavigation. Clusius did not ask about gold. Perhaps he knew there was no point. Or perhaps the gold is just not what the expedition's success *meant* to him. 'God gave each plant strength to live, and each plant teaches us about His presence,' he once wrote.

He observes that Drake's sailors had brought cocoa beans from the coast of Peru. One of them showed him a piece of 'dragon root', which he said the Spanish settlers 'would not part with for any price' on account of its medicinal powers. Drake himself gave him a *bezoar* stone. John Winter, commander of the *Elizabeth*, which sailed through the Straits of Magellan before becoming separated from the main expedition and sailing home, gave him a specimen of the bark he had found in Patagonia, which he had used to cure his crew of scurvy.

The breadfruit and the land crabs and the fireflies they'd seen in the Spice Islands, the papyrus they'd brought back from Java: all were duly written up by this Frenchman who evidently hadn't noticed that the circumnavigation was about politics and economics and nothing else. The reference to Javan papyrus is particularly intriguing – it was 'the white bark of a tree . . . a very slender membrane, which took every kind of writing.' The city on Java at which they called after the mishap off Celebes had been an important Hindu and Buddhist centre in its time and would soon be Muslim: this was a highly literate society. Clusius recorded that Drake's crew went to some lengths to obtain these exotic writing materials 'in exchange for other commodities.'

Clusius must have realised that he was, in his quiet way, breaking the embargo on what the world was allowed to know about the voyage. Perhaps the government considered such information harmless, or a useful distraction, even, from the 'main business' of the venture. Perhaps they saw it as merely a variation on the gushing eulogies which had also appeared in Drake's honour. But there is nothing to suggest that the crew themselves saw these plants as a 'distraction'. They had mattered enough that they wanted to collect them, get them home and discuss them with a botanist once they got there.

Those who have studied Clusius' letters most closely have been struck by how extensive his contacts were. His Europe-wide network, at a time of heightened religious and political tensions, transcended all such divides. Science, or 'natural philosophy', had not yet been professionalised. Clusius was in regular contact with people across religious, class and gender divisions. He translated from Spanish and, as we've seen, corresponded with English and German collectors alike. He had lived in Hungary. He had botanised in the hills around Bristol.

'At a time when most of Europe was locked in war over matters of religion and imperial ambition,' the historian Deborah Harkness has written, 'the exchange of natural objects prompted an intellectual civility that stood in stark contrast to national disputes.' The audience for his account of Drake's journey was international and intellectually curious. Such an audience may have been deemed insignificant by the English government of the day and some historians may still, four centuries later, feel obliged to go along with that verdict. The rest of us are free to find significance as and where we please.

———

Those centuries have taken their toll on the Exeter Cathedral archive's copy. I replace the rubber bands holding it together, wondering how I could have missed this place for so long. The book I've been looking at is one of a large collection donated by an 18th-century Exeter physician. I see from the catalogue that it includes early editions of Gesner, Galileo, Kepler and Descartes, as well as Renaissance editions of Galen and Aristotle. I don't consciously decide that lunch can wait but I ask for a biography of the man who put this collection together and begin to read.

Thomas Glass's portrait still hangs at the Royal Devon and Exeter Hospital, where he was a doctor from its foundation in 1741. His most acclaimed work was in the development of a smallpox vaccine. For this he was made an associate of the Royal Society of Medicine in Paris in 1776. But he found time, also, to write a six hundred-page commentary on an ancient Roman physician. He had mineral baths installed at the hospital and wrote about their medical benefits, as described by ancient authorities.

How can I have been skipping in and out of Exeter all these years and never heard about this? I comfort myself that this is just the right moment to chance upon him. I wouldn't have had the question before to which this collection is such an excellent answer. I made further appointments in the weeks that followed to see more.

I haven't space here to do justice to the riches of this archive. There is the magnificently illustrated second edition of Vesalius' *Fabric of the Human Body*, which transformed the study of anatomy. There is an early edition of John Dee's *The Hieroglyphic Monad*, a Hermetic treatise. But Conrad Gesner's work is perhaps the most relevant here. Born in Zurich, Gesner was read all over Europe in the 1550s. He was a well-travelled man and a gifted linguist, in constant communication, like Clusius, with people right across the continent. There is perhaps no better illustration of this dispute between the old world and the emergent one than his *History of Animals*. It was a compendium of everything that had ever been written about each animal, by ancient zoologists, by historians, poets or medical men.

The index of animal names is in five different European languages plus Greek, Hebrew, Persian and Arabic. Exeter's copy belonged, in the 17th century, to a college in Moravia, where someone has added words in Hungarian here and there. The main text is, of course, in Latin, the international lingua franca of the day.

With Gesner we are, unmistakably, in the thick of a transformative moment: the embattled state of understanding is everywhere. Sphynxes are to be found in Transylvania (why is it always Transylvania?) but for unicorns you have to go to India. A sea snake is shown in the act of devouring an entire ship, for scale. After the flying fishes come marine creatures which look just like little monks, then others which look like little bishops. And I suppose to most people in the 1550s, if you could believe that fish can fly, then why would you not also believe that the oceans are teeming with toy clergymen?

Yet turn another page and Gesner is one of us entirely. His blackbird, say, is every inch the one I'm familiar with from my own chimney pot on summer evenings. The stork comes complete with a serpent struggling in its bill and may well be pointing a moral, but this is beyond question a real stork, too. Gesner's birds of prey are especially jealous of this new free-dom to be themselves. They puff out their feathers and glare indignantly. Escaped from that cage of heraldic poses which has held them so long captive, they are not about to be lured back into anybody's coat of arms.

Few witnesses to 'the great unsettling' are so elo-quent about its effect upon relations with the natural world. But with him the dispute is in its early stages.

Galileo was still under house arrest when Exeter's copy of the book for which he was tried, *A Dialogue Concerning the World's Two Chief World Systems*, was printed. His dialogue pits a defender of ancient authority against an advocate of the new learning. Johannes Kepler's book about Copernicus, also in the collection, was also written in question and answer form.

The Renaissance was an argument and this archive is a great place to eavesdrop on it. Any weekday you will find students or university teachers or independent scholars quietly consulting the collections. I didn't think reading-rooms like this still existed. The glass-fronted book-cases are loaded with history and theology. At its far end sits the top half of Richard II's head, in limestone. Stolen from the cathedral's west front, he had already been replaced by the time this part of the original was recovered from a skip in Torrington. In his new context he appears as a dream king or as the illustration of a paradox, rising forever solemnly out of his window-sill and forever sinking back into it.

PART THREE

– Fetching the Future Home –

THE BURNING OR GLITTERING LIGHT
OF THE SEA

Francis Fletcher's narrative tells what it calls 'A strange stoary of Birds'. I've already quoted a little of it. On arrival at the east coast of South America, what was still a small fleet was hit by severe storms, but they sailed on past the River Plate. There they came upon a 'faire & large Iland' which proved to be 'a stoare house of victuals for a King's army . . . such was the infinite stoare of Eggs & birdes.'

Fletcher clearly made one of the party which went ashore. The birds were so thick on the ground that they could only respond by flying up to sit on the 'heads shoulders armes' of these unexpected visitors. In Fletcher's account, this first phase is actually very touching, given that the reader knows, as the penguins clearly did not, what this landing party had come for.

Once the killing starts the mood quickly changes: 'no beating with Poles, cudgels swords & daggers would keep them ofe . . . till with pulling and killing we fainted.' The mariners were beaten back by the sheer number of panicking birds, but Fletcher records that they later returned 'to take revenge upon so barbarous adversaryes.' Fletcher saw 'barbarous adversaries' in all the places where 16th-century Englishmen expected to find them. He tore down Catholic shrines. He may have enjoyed the music in Patagonia but he wrote up their religion as devil worship.

So isn't what I've attempted here a kind of special pleading? What if these lesser known figures of mine, so wrongly overlooked, were in fact fully implicated? I described earlier a large whale that was encountered on the second attempt to reach Asia by the north-east route. William Borough was in that 40-foot boat and would have been twenty at the time – then as now an impressionable age. Bowheads regularly reach 60 feet in length. A document he produced twenty years later would suggest that this early fright left its mark.

The tone is no longer religious awe or any other kind. Its title is *A note of all the necessary instruments and appurtenances belonging to the killing of the Whale.* It details 'how many harping irons, speares, cordes, axes, hatchets, knives, and other implements for the fishing' are needed. How many 'pullies to turn the Whale', how many 'furnaces to melt the Whale in.' Another three decades would pass before the Royal Muscovy Company began to hunt commercially in these waters. But over the next three centuries, the British whaling industry would play its part in driving the northern bowhead whale to the verge of extinction.

The darker side of this only gets darker but by denying it we make it available to those who then fasten upon this as the essence of the whole enterprise. Carl Schmitt, for example, the Nazi legal theorist, was a keen admirer of the Elizabethan explorers and much interested in their West Country connections. He thrilled to these 'corsair capitalists', all partners together in 'the big business of plunder.' He chose to see the rapacious nationalism and the nascent imperialism and nothing else. Schmitt, it's worth recalling, was a strong influence on key advisers to the Putin administration, particularly on foreign relations. But this isn't all about those pesky 'Rooshans and Prooshans': even that family of eccentrics I began with, living the simple life on their Devon hill-top, were at one time close to the British Fascist movement. Their motives in setting up that plaster statue may well have been 'patriotic' to a degree that would make most 'patriots' uneasy.

It matters how we remember this. Drake took part in slaving voyages as a young man and this remains an indelible mark against his name. It's also true he later returned to the Caribbean and made common cause with communities of escaped slaves. No doubt he did so from strategic considerations and out of self-interest. But he appears to have formed an enduring friendship with one of them: might this not suggest some possible awareness, at the very least, of a terrible wrong inflicted?

As with the low points of his career, so with the highest: for popular historians even today, the circumnavigation is almost invariably framed as a national achievement, then praised or condemned according to taste. But how 'national' was it in fact? Drake's charts were Dutch, Portuguese and Spanish. The pilots he used were Portuguese, Greek or they were indigenous. There were French, Scottish, Basque, Afro-Caribbean, Dutch and Danish crew members.

Drake's cousin John, captured later by the Spanish, would describe Francis to the Inquisition as 'a native of Menguen a hundred leagues from London.' Was this deliberate nonsense or a translator's struggle with some mumbled version of 'Devon'? It certainly doesn't sound much like Tavistock, which is where he was actually from. Scribal error or wily stratagem, being from 'Menguen' came nearer than anyone ever had to being from nowhere.

Even as the explorers underwent these new forms of disorientation they were disagreeing about what it meant. Not as we might have, because they could not yet know what would follow from their actions. That 'infinite stoare' which they all saw, of penguins or whales or seals or cod, really did appear to be infinite. So of course the birds which rested on the ship in mid-ocean 'had been comanded of God to yield themselves to be meat for us.' No 16th-century chaplain had ever heard of anthropology: of course the natives are devil-worshippers. With the historical record, as with our own pasts, to remember is so often to look back on how we didn't get it at the time. And be mocked by a voice which says: *So you do now?* What history teaches us is to hear that mocking voice.

Back in 1556, the crew of the *Searchthrift*, throwing snow out of their ship 'with shovels in August', ran into storms. The 'great and terrible abundance of ice which we saw with our eies', soon forced the tiny vessel back. Tracking west at the end of August, they sailed straight through the waters where the Prirazlomnoye Platform is currently moored, its multiple wells 'bringing on line' the first oil from beneath the Arctic shelf. According to Gazprom, the millionth tonne of Russian Arctic oil was extracted in November 2015. The product is quite heavy but suitable for road-building, car tyres and pharmaceuticals.

It was, notoriously, not friendly fishermen who greeted the Greenpeace activists when they set out to draw the world's attention to this development. Thirty of them were arrested and then held at gunpoint as their ship was towed into Murmansk. In the charge of 'piracy' that was brought against them, the echo of an earlier age played round the edges of this story. The suggestion, though, that Greenpeace was trying to get its hands on Gazprom's oil revenue was far-fetched even by the standards of Kremlin TV. Before the storm of international condemnation which followed, even the Arctic calculus of a Vladimir Putin was forced to retreat. The hostages were released.

But this was not the first time Greenpeace's attention had been drawn to the area. The population of

Novaya Zemlya was relocated in 1954 and their island home, which bounds the Pechora Sea to the east, was renamed 'The Novaya Zemlya Test Site'. This was Russia's Maralinga or Bikini Atoll. More than two hundred nuclear detonations were carried out on the island, including the largest human-made explosion in history, carried out in 1961. Their combined force has been calculated to be more than a hundred times that of all the explosives used during the Second World War, the atom bombs included. Two nuclear submarines and an estimated 17,000 containers of radioactive waste are still lying in its offshore waters.

That is all history now, of course. And it is forty years since Jan Patočka died in police custody. Gazprom continues to drill and the news cycle continues to spin. 'Our' version spins this story as Russia vs the rest, and little wonder. But other test sites in other 'remote' corners of the earth tell their own tales. British, Dutch and American oil companies were among the most eager to lend their Russian counterparts assistance in the Arctic.

It was in these very waters that the earliest explorers, equipped with the latest technology, encountered great whales and later fatefully speculated about how oil might most efficiently be extracted from them. That conjunction may raise questions too knotty for the newsroom but are they therefore to be left unasked?

What Greenpeace and the world were encountering in the Pechora Sea in 2013 is a problem deeply rooted in historical paradox. And to that paradox the news cycle is worse than a poor guide. It often seems to function, rather, as a purpose-built distraction, designed to delay (or, ideally, to cancel) our ever posing the real questions at all. 'We speak of the danger as if it were not ourselves,' as Adrienne Rich once put it.

To this day, to take another of my 'unjustly neglected' figures, the British claim John Davis as the discoverer of the Falkland Islands. Even the doughtiest of UK passport holders must concede that he was hopelessly lost at the time. And he can hardly be held responsible for everything that has followed. But did he or did he not also captain the first expedition of the East India Company? He did. And as it happens he also wrote about what he thought the ultimate purpose of these voyages was or ought to be.

In a treatise on the art of navigation, which he returned to his home by the Dart to write in the 1590s, he argued that it was a practise both 'speculative' and 'mechanicall'. Most of the treatise is given over to the latter, to explaining the new technology – Davis was the inventor of a new kind of quadrant. He explained not only how such devices worked but why they mattered, too. By the 'exceeding great hazards' of those who put to sea, he wrote, 'excellent benefites are atchieved . . . the forme of the earth, the quantities of Countries, the diuersitie of nations and the natures of Zones, Climats, Countries and people, are apparently made known unto us.'

Navigation, he wrote, echoing Robert Norman, 'is the meane whereby Countreyes are discouered, and communitie drawne between nation and nation . . .' Of the North-West passage he writes specifically: 'The benefits which may grow by this discovery are copious, and of two sorts – a benefit spirituall and a benefit corporall. Both which . . . by the laws of God and nature we are bound to regard . . .'

Is it for us to convict him of hypocrisy? Davis's references, you might argue, to the 'great store of whales' he encountered in the North Atlantic, these are a better guide. He wasn't expressing naïve admiration. When he said 'store', he knew, as Fletcher did, exactly what he was saying. And I agree. He probably did. When he brought back quantities of cod from the same expedition, he clearly meant to attract investors. He assumed that the world's abundance was inexhaustible. And we know now that he was wrong. But the real point for us is surely a question and the question is, for we who *do* now know, what shall we make of that knowledge?

—

In February 2015, two women walking on a beach in the Isles of Scilly watched and photographed a 25-foot whale close inshore. They were concerned at first that it might be stranded, but after fifteen minutes or so it swam away. They had noticed the whale had no dorsal fin and the images were circulated. It was identified by local naturalists as a sperm whale. But when the photographs were sent to a specialist, the shape of the head and the jaw-line seemed wrong to him. He sent them on to colleagues in North America, who confirmed that this was in fact a young bowhead whale.

That this creature was unfamiliar to British naturalists is only to be expected: this was in fact its first recorded sighting in UK waters. They are normally found in the high Arctic but semi-fossilised remains in North Sea sediments show they were present there at the end of the last Ice Age. So this sighting was the first sign of their presence this far south for around 11,000 years. A second was sighted close inshore off mainland Cornwall in May 2016 and probably the same one re-appeared off Brittany shortly afterwards.

You might be wondering why, at a time of warming oceans, such a creature would head south? It may be that as the Arctic ice retreats, so zooplankton have found ideal conditions, so that baleen whales, like the bowhead, are, paradoxically, flourishing.

Bowheads can live for up to two hundred years and demonstrated this in spectacular, if gruesome fashion, when an iron arrowhead dating from the 19th century was found embedded deep inside the tissues of a whale as it was butchered by Inuit in 2007. Their genome has been sequenced, uniquely among sea mammals, for any clues it may offer to the secret of their longevity – they are, after the Greenland shark, the longest-lived creatures on earth. These visitors to European waters now, in other words, could be only three or four generations on from the giants that so unnerved Davis and Borough. What they could not have known, we do. So what, then, do we *make* of these sightings?

Before we make anything of them, another, less mysterious, conjecture also belongs in this mix. Most of the major American and European oil companies own licenses to explore and exploit the sea bed off North-eastern Greenland. Over the last five years, therefore, the usual habitat of bowhead whales has been exposed for the first time to 'seismic blasting'. This is carried out by specialist vessels along a 5000 mile 'survey line'. Essentially each vessel tows an array of air guns which repeatedly blast low frequency sound-waves at the sea bed. By 'reading' the echo they can detect oil-bearing sediments. Above water each of those blasts would be perceived by humans as about sixty times louder than a shot gun 1 metre away.

If we shudder, now, at William Borough and his 'necessary instruments', at John Davis and his 'great store' of whales, what in our own times comes closest to such attitudes? Perhaps what we should be marvelling at is that the appearance of such a creature made so little impression. In the news economy, it was swiftly graded as at best an intriguing snippet. Local story. In any world intent upon making sense, surely those sightings would have been just the occasion to wonder how far those bad old assumptions have not gone away at all but simply camouflaged themselves? Or are we perverse and quibbling heretics for even suggesting such a possibility?

———

Neither was it serious news, when, also in 2015, just below the house where John Davis grew up, the last nets were set for salmon on the River Dart. To Davis, that silver haul being dragged ashore would have been a familiar sight. And he would have known as well as anyone else in such a community that salmon come from the sea.

The last of those netsmen was paid off in 2015 and the commercial salmon fishery on the Dart, long in decline, officially ceased to exist. Climate change is driving their prey species ever further north and mortality at sea has increased. The conservationists who managed this closure argue that we need to think of wild Atlantic salmon as a resource no longer, but rather as an iconic species, as an indicator of planetary health.

Much about the route they take on their migration remains a mystery, but West Country fish make for the waters east and west of Greenland. The John Davis, in other words, who 'shaped his course northwards' from the Scillies four centuries and more ago, could not have known that in doing so he was following the migratory route of the very fish on which his home community depended. Another two hundred years would pass before their Arctic feeding-grounds became known.

There is so much we know, too late. Recent studies

show that migrating salmon generally travel close to the surface, which may permit them to steer by the stars. In the open sea, they are certainly guided by the earth's magnetic field, picking up on the scent of individual rivers only as they approach the coast. Davis was a fine navigator and astronomer. Would he have been amazed to learn that salmon had got there first? But perhaps salmon, even from his home river, were just one more commodity of which the world had 'great store', one more abundance 'so great that we knew not the limits thereof.'

To vilify gets us no closer than the old sentimentalities did. They were divided, among themselves as each within himself. It may be for us to trace the lines along which they divided. It is not for us to assume that the hunger for understanding, when they claimed it as a main motive, was hypocrisy.

Preserved at Hatfield House is a chart of the North Atlantic made by William Borough in 1576. Most of it is empty space. It is at first sight a puzzling document. Borough delivered it to his customer, Martin Frobisher, with the coastlines of Holland, eastern England, Scotland, northern Ireland and western Scandinavia drawn in. From a star-burst in mid-Atlantic thirty-two compass rays extend over the ocean. Frobisher has filled in the coastlines he explored on the other side, so this 'chart of the North Atlantic' in fact shows only one bay in the Canadian Arctic and the southern tip of Greenland. Everything else is left blank.

Quite apart from its value as a historical document, this is richly suggestive of how the world looked to these people. Other islands, rumoured to exist by earlier travellers, are there in pencil, presumably for their outlines to be inked in if they were actually found to exist. They weren't there and are now so faint that they are only visible using infra-red light. The ship's course is traceable, arrows showing where readings of magnetic variation were taken. Otherwise all is an expert mesh of rhumb-lines. This is a map made by people who are very well aware of how much they still have to learn.

On his very last voyage, in 1605, John Davis noted the following in his log, as the ship passed Ascension Island:

The twelfth of February, wee found ourselves to bee in seven degrees five minutes to the South-ward [of the Equator]; in which place at night, I thinke I saw the strangest Sea that ever was seene: which was, That the burning or glittering light of the Sea did shew to us, as though all the Sea over had beene burning flames of fire; and all night long, the Moone being downe, you might see to read in any booke by the light thereof . . .

What he saw, incidentally, was also seen by Darwin in the South Atlantic two hundred and thirty years later. Darwin, too, was deeply moved.

DOING THE SUMS

The yellow dots track the movements of a tagged seal, 'rs9-832-11', in the Canadian High Arctic. It turns circles in Prince Regent Inlet through November and December, then travels east along the coast of Devon Island. It dives regularly for fish, to between a hundred and two hundred metres beneath the sea ice. Back at the surface, the electronic tag is programmed to select the best moment for transmission of the data it has gathered. Entering Baffin Bay in January, the seal turns south into the Davis Straits. By early summer it is off the Cumberland Peninsula. Transmissions cease.

The sensor, glued to the hair on its forehead, drops off in the early summer moult. The seal is quite unharmed and in the course of its journey rs9-832-11 transmitted more than four hundred profiles over 228 days. Researchers from ten different countries are collaborating on the project in which this creature was participating unawares. Such animal-borne devices are now used regularly to explore ocean currents beneath the sea-ice.

Designed originally to help biologists study the foraging behaviour of seals, it was quickly realised that their movements through the water column, with some species diving to a depth of 2000 metres, made them the ideal 'explorers' of this marine system as a whole. The tags can now be made inexpensively and the Arctic is changing faster than any environment on the planet. Due to the retreating ice-cover, waters from the North Pacific are now mixing with those of the North Atlantic for the first time in thousands of years, with consequences that nobody can predict.

John Davis noted the 'marveilous great abundance of seales' in the strait which today bears his name. By and large it took us several centuries to think of these creatures as more than a marvellous great supply of meat and skins. But we discovered a richer kind of relationship with them in the end. We have never needed to know more urgently what is going on under the ice and, especially in winter, seals are a cost-effective way of finding out.

—

Traffic into Exeter from the east, watched over by speed cameras, slows at a series of complicated junctions. The Met Office, with its Hadley Centre for the Study of Climate Change, nestles here by the motorway, well out of sight among the slip-roads and the superstores, the garages and depots. It was moved down from the outskirts of London about fifteen years ago. Set in its own miniature park, at the end of its own miniature drive, it is all plate glass and brilliantly lit interior spaces, a gleaming show-case for the government's commitment to climate science. This is where they do the sums.

Over a coffee, I am given a kind of backstage tour of the shipping forecast. The head of Marine

Observations tells me about their array of satellites, buoys, radar installations, tide gauges and submersibles. Those seals crop up as part of a discussion about how such networks of observation are coming under pressure as government funding is cut. Closer to home, sensors are being fitted to lobster pots and fishing nets as new technology offers more cost-effective ways to study inshore waters.

Since the Paris agreement, his department, Ocean Forecasting, has funding to provide detailed information, from 2018, on how higher levels of atmospheric CO_2 are likely to affect marine habitats in particular localities around the UK. For 'Copernicus', a Europe-wide programme, it leads the monitoring of the 'North West European Continental Shelf', analysing data provided by all the other countries involved and producing forecasts. Salinity, surface temperature, currents, wind, waves, sea-level, plankton, algae blooms – all of these are continually monitored and models are devised to combine these observations.

Take 'sea surface temperature' as just one example. We all know what that means. It's the difference between whether we go in or not. But if you are studying exchange processes between the atmosphere and the ocean, what matters is a layer between 10 and 20 microns thick, the 'surface microlayer', a kind of skin stretching right across the ocean. It accounts for the glassy stillness that we sometimes observe on calm days. For others, looking at plankton, say, it might be the top 10 centimetres that matter. For others again 'bulk' sea surface temperature, the top 2 metres of the water column, is what counts. The head of Ocean Forecasting puts it like this: 'On a hot still day in Lyme Bay there will be big differences between these, depending where you are in the water and what instruments you are using. Finding the way to model that complexity is especially important for climate records. Variation between seasons is very clear. The variations that matter for climate are much smaller.'

—

Balearic shearwaters began to be noticed more regularly in Lyme Bay in the early years of this century. Shearwaters, of all birds among the best conservers of energy, alternate a rapid flickering with long glides on stiffly outstretched wings, keeping very low over the sea. The Manx shearwater, the most familiar around British shores, actually spends the first three or four years of its life off the coast of Argentina, thereafter migrating each year the full length of the Atlantic and back again. They can live for up to fifty years.

The Balearic is very closely related but is restricted in its range, or was until recently, to the western Mediterranean and Biscay. Its rarity and the shift in its feeding-grounds due to climate change made them an object of close study. The naturalist Tom Brereton, a founder member of the citizen science initiative MARINElife, researched their arrival in Lyme Bay.

Accompanying fishermen as they went about their work, he quickly began to build up a detailed picture of many other creatures that frequent the bay.

One discovery above all stands out. Lyme Bay is deepest in the central western area, where much of the sea-bed is more than 50 metres below the surface. On one trip the boat was accompanied by dolphins which looked a little strange to him. They seemed to have a white band across the top of their beaks. At first he wondered if this was some trick of the light. He kept watching. It wasn't. Back home he went online and looked through clips of bow-riding dolphins taken by holiday-makers yachting in Lyme Bay. Several of them showed what he had just seen.

You would not look for white-beaked dolphins in Lyme Bay. They are a creature more associated with the Arctic. It was recently observed, in fact, that one response of polar bears to the loss of sea ice has been to switch prey species. White-beaked dolphin is figuring more and more regularly in their diet. They do occur in the North Sea and there are some in Biscay, but the surprising presence of a year-round population in Lyme Bay must be linked to the cooler water in its deepest areas, where the cod and whiting it relies on are most plentiful, especially around wrecks.

In conjunction with Exeter University, Tom arranged to fix a hydrophone to one of these wrecks, in order to record and study their communications. It spent a summer down there before Tom arranged for a TV personality and the BBC to be there when divers retrieved it. The day before, he wanted to check whether any dolphins were around and likely to play along. An international tour company had recently included the white-beaks as an eco-attraction, so Tom was able to treat this reconnaissance trip as both a commercial venture and an opportunity to clock up further records for the MARINElife database. Here were research and awareness-raising, simultaneously being funded through eco-tourism. Don't tell me it can't be done.

When he rang up one Friday evening to ask if I could do the bird-surveying, I didn't need to be asked twice. The group of global birders were waiting for us on the quay next morning. 'Eco-tourists' doesn't quite do justice to them. They sported a variety of gigantic lenses, several of them finished with camouflage paint. These were birders who had been everywhere and seen everything, or almost. They were serious and they had, as Tom only now informed me with a nervous laugh, not yet paid. The white-beaks had better be in the mood to oblige.

We set out under clear skies into a warm southerly breeze. Portland, fifteen miles away across the bay, even at that distance takes up a good chunk of the horizon. On a clear day like this, the earth's curvature seems to leave the lighthouse at its southern tip stranded a short way out to sea. Strange that I should have returned to this of all coastlines. But moving back here felt like a natural progression in some way I didn't need to explain.

The top of the wheel house had been converted into a look-out. I climbed the ladder and took up position as we left the harbour. There was a puffin before too long and then a red-throated diver. There were swallows a long way out and terns. It was not for these that the global birders had come. Gannets bobbed in vast white rafts spread out around the fishing boats we passed: they too seemed to be waiting for something else. The three species of skuas accompanying them suggested that these were birds travelling south from Scotland or further north.

A sooty shearwater went by, early forerunner of the vast flocks which pass through the Channel each autumn, *en route* from the Arctic to the South Atlantic. Their range is even more spectacular than the Manx. Some of them even pass from there into the Pacific. At least as global as any global birder, the sooty met with some grudging respect.

My role was to identify birds and note the time of each sighting. Using the ship's GPS, the exact positions are later mapped relative to that sea surface temperature we've already met, as well as to salinity, chlorophyll, sea depth, presence of wrecks, etc. And with one thing and another I'd not been out on the water lately as much as I'd have liked to be. So this was a much-needed 'reminder' of that other dimension that is there all the time, running parallel to my daily life. As so many of us do, I need contact with that other world, to which my own is just a shadow on the northern horizon. To be out there was to see that everyday bit of blue in-fill on my horizon expanded to its proper dimensions.

And sooty shearwaters, after all, were veterans of that wider world long before we knew anything about it or them. Knowing even the little we do now already makes short work of our claim, as a species, to have 'discovered' the world in the 16th century or at any other time for that matter. These dark skittering silhouettes would have reeled and banked around the explorers and the cod fishermen alike. And here they were now, on the same long, bowed wings, sailing right along the southern edge of my world.

It was, in short, getting a bit trippy up there in my look-out. I had brought a sun-hat but perhaps I had inhaled a little more blue than was good for me. Either way, the paperwork was a steadying influence as we entered the west of the bay. There had been several false alarms and we were well into the afternoon without any sightings, more or less south of Exeter and several miles out.

A pod surfacing nearby broke the tension: six or seven of them in a row, blowing together then gone again. Just that glimpse triggered stampeding to starboard. A long pause followed. Had they scared at the sight of us? Was that it? Did this count as a sighting at all? They put our minds at rest by re-surfacing close enough that the boat could be nudged in their direction. They were diving a well-known wreck and quite as preoccupied as the anglers who visit the same wreck for the same reason. Only a calf paid us any attention, twice veering off from the main group to try and bow-ride, twice fetched back by an adult.

But they gave us twenty minutes or so. The famous white noses, each time they appeared, were greeted with a chorus of continuous photo drives. Our haul for the day was secure: it was with relief that we turned east again, but with gratitude, also, that the white-beaks had sympathised with our predicament.

———

Estate agents call it a 'sea-glimpse', by which they mean the poor relation of a sea-view. But moving back to the West Country, re-decorating upstairs, I rejoiced in my fragment of blue horizon lost among the roof-tops and the telephone wires. Walking across fields to a beach beat walking down a street to the Thames any day. My new neighbours told me about the winter months when you can hear the waves thumping into the coastal defences more than a mile away and I heard it myself soon enough.

But awareness of just how much was going on in Lyme Bay dawned slowly. Through some combination of loyalty and laziness, I never had, in my years of travel, got around to cancelling that subscription to the Devon Wildlife Trust. I'd joined at twelve, just after my recruitment to bird-watching. Its magazine landed on the doormat of my new home not long after I moved back and I read it more carefully than usual. I learnt about the long-standing campaign for a ban on scallop-dredging in Lyme Bay. And I began to pay closer attention to these new surroundings of mine.

Moving back to the South West had made relatively little difference, until then, to what I wrote about. I went on travelling a lot for magazines. But that article about Lyme Bay had my immediate attention. I should perhaps explain from the outset that a scallop dredge is a row of steel spikes which is dragged across the sea-bed ahead of a chain mail bag. It is, in effect, a set of metal teeth with a very large stomach in tow. The damage caused by this fishing method has been exhaustively documented. If you wanted an image for everything that is wrong about our relationship with the sea, you could do a lot worse than a scallop dredge.

Lyme Bay, stretching from Portland in the east to Start Point in the west, encloses roughly six hundred square miles of in-shore waters. Daniel Defoe passed through West Bay in 1722:

we saw Boats all the way on the Shore fishing for *Mackerell*, which they take in the easiest Manner imaginable . . . the Men haling the Net to the Shore at both Ends, bring with it such Fish as they surrounded [in boats] . . . this, at that Time, proved to be an incredible Number, insomuch that the Men could hardly draw them on Shore . . . Such was the Plenty of

Fish that Year that the *Mackerell*, the finest and largest I ever saw, were sold at the Sea-side a hundred for a Penny.

They were still being netted in this way off Chesil Beach well within living memory – there are photographs of it on the walls of pubs. Industrial fishing long ago put paid to such scenes and the introduction of spring-loaded dredges in the 1970s and 1980s finally brought the bay's limestone reefs within reach. The damage being done to sponges, pink sea fans and cold water corals was first documented by a diver and photographer called Colin Munroe in 1992. He sent images to the Devon Wildlife Trust, which published them in its magazine and raised the alarm.

The problem was already serious, even before the price of diesel started rising. More boats than ever were soon attracted to a fishery which cost so little to reach. There was no quota on scallops and TV chefs had made them popular. I had already been looking for a way to involve myself in this campaign when the MS *Napoli*, a large cargo ship, obliged me by starting to break up during a winter gale early in 2007. Deliberately run aground in Lyme Bay so that it could be salvaged, about a hundred of the containers stacked on its deck were lost overboard. A few of them washed up on a nearby beach and were looted.

The campaign of a local Wildlife Trust to stop scallop-dredging is not news, as several magazine editors had already pointed out to me, but an oil-spill was and so was this horde of latter-day wreckers. Welcome to what sells magazines. In the guise of writing about the news, I finally got to write about what really interested me. There were several people I'd been wanting a pretext to interview – fishermen, biologists, activists. Here was my chance.

It felt perverse, of course, to view such an occasion as an 'opportunity', but such is the logic of the current affairs industry. I'd claimed, in other contexts, to be looking for a way to live and write that didn't mean jumping in aeroplanes quite so regularly – well . . .

The government was already taking scientific advice on how much of our coastal waters should be protected if fish stocks were to stand some chance of recovery. The advice was: about one third. In Lyme Bay, several 'voluntary agreements' with fishermen had been tried, but none of these succeeded in excluding the largest and most damaging dredgers, mainly from Wales and the Isle of Man.

When the government consulted, I wrote the response for a local environmental group. Such consultations of course rarely have much effect, so I was astonished when the government decided to make of Lyme Bay a test case. In July 2008, a Statutory Instrument protecting its sea-bed from all towed fishing gear was announced by the Secretary of State in Lyme Regis. Sixty square miles of the bay were designated, far and away the largest such reserve ever created in UK waters. Another thirty miles were added in 2009 under European legislation, a further fifteen by the British Government in 2013.

Given the scale of the site, surveying its recovery presented challenges. But all agree that the sea-bed has recovered quickly, even on the loose sandy gravels between reefs where little or no change had been expected. Ross coral, branching sponges and sea fans have all recovered strongly, as have scallops and lobsters. Allow the sea some time and the surprises soon begin.

Small boats have signed up to an agreement, initially brokered by the Blue Marine Foundation, whereby they limit their catch in the common interest and police the protected areas against any dredging. All larger vessels must now carry inshore Vessel Monitoring Systems. Mobile phone networks will soon be used to track smaller vessels and the Inshore Fisheries and Conservation Authorities also have patrol boats and radar. The port of Brixham, in Lyme Bay, was, in the 17th century, one of the first in Britain to employ the then new (and already controversial) technology of bottom trawling. Four centuries on, the 'technological creep', which has for so long worked against marine habitats, is finally being used to protect them.

The time for euphoria is, as usual, not yet. The scientific advice on which the Protected Area was set up was for 30 per cent of the UK's inshore waters to be No Take Zones, i.e. areas in which no fishing at all takes place. That may have been unrealistic but there still is not one solitary square mile of No Take Zone in Lyme

Bay or in any of the other more recent designations. Indeed, of the 750,000 square kilometres of the UK's coastal waters, 7.5 square kilometres, a one hundred thousandth part of that area, is fully protected.

After a consultation involving more than a million people and the government's own scientific advisors, costing almost £10m, a network of 127 Marine Conservation Zones was proposed in 2010, in which certain forms of fishing would be banned. In sixty-five additional 'reference areas' no fishing would take place. The reference areas were all later dropped and just fifty of the 127 sites proposed have become reserves. The scientific body commissioned to advise on this, The Royal Commission on Environmental Pollution, was meanwhile abolished in 2010 by a Conservative government which had come to power on promises to be 'the greenest government ever'.

LIFE ON BOARD THE *EXETER*

Fisheries scientists have long argued that Marine Protected Areas (MPAs) have never been shown to work outside the Tropics. There is a growing body of scientific evidence, however, that they do exactly what you would expect them to do, in temperate waters as elsewhere. They result in larger numbers of older, larger, more fertile fish, which then improve fish stocks in the surrounding area through 'spill-over'. This has been demonstrated for coastal populations of cod in Scandinavia, as well as for lobsters and scallops in UK coastal waters.

MPAs are not, of course, opposed because they don't work. They plainly do. They are opposed because they represent an alternative to the short-termism by which the industry and its friends in government choose to be guided.

What is true of MPAs is even truer of No Take Zones. Their purpose is the recovery of a habitat to something like its condition prior to industrial exploitation. The campaigning for them, and then the recovery itself, take time. Neither will the recovery ever be entirely 'as expected'. In January 2014, Lyme Bay was hit by three storms of a magnitude that would normally be expected every fifty years. Scientists already studying the bay's recovery were able to look at how it was impacted by the kind of extreme weather event we can expect more of in the future. In other words, work undertaken to study a Protected Area was now telling us what we can expect from climate change, too.

Tracking such changes is only possible in areas which have been permanently closed to certain fishing methods or to all fishing. Without such areas, we can't know 'what the sea might regenerate towards.' And this is the nub of it: the reason Protected Areas are opposed by the industrial fishing lobby is because they represent a long-term commitment to understanding marine habitats.

That 'long-term commitment' is about their future prospects of course but not only that. Researchers have also analysed official catch data, i.e. records of fish landed, which for the Channel go back to the 1920s. The fishing industry bases its own assessment of stock on the same data but cry foul when environmentalists use them, too, as the basis of their own studies. The catch data strongly suggest a massive shift to reduced biodiversity over the past century. And the offence caused by this finding is only compounded by other discoveries being made.

What we describe as 'industrial fishing' began with the introduction of steam trawling in the mid-19th century, so you need to go back well beyond the 1920s. Biologists are picking through the accounts of travellers, not to mention explorers, in search of a pre-industrial baseline against which the present state of our seas can be measured. They have picked through medieval laws and trade agreements. They are searching the archaeological record, too, for clues to what our seas were like before industrial fishing got its teeth into them.

Aelfric's Colloquy is one example of how their approach might work for the Dorset coastline. This 'colloquy', or discussion, arose from a teaching experiment devised by a monk at Cerne Abbas in the 10th century. Trying to interest novices in learning Latin, Aelfric interviewed people from all walks of life: a ploughman, a shepherd and a hunter, a lawyer, a merchant and a cook. Aelfric translated his questions and their answers into Latin, then set his pupils to translate these back into Anglo-Saxon. His interviews are about as close as we will ever get to a fly-on-the-wall documentary about everyday life in Anglo-Saxon England.

He also interviewed a fisherman from somewhere near Wareham. The interview includes a fascinating exchange about the dangers of hunting for whales in the English Channel, which makes it quite clear that they were at that time abundant in the West Country's coastal waters. Not to mention the oysters, herring, sturgeon, dolphin and salmon of which there were also no shortages. It can only follow from this that there existed, at that time, marine (and river) habitats which were able to sustain all of this.

The response to evidence of this kind from industry scientists is that since we do not have scientific data from the pre-scientific era, it follows that such evidence as we do have must be discounted. Especially when it tends to suggest that having Marine Protected Areas might be a rather good idea. The industry's preferred time-frame is both shorter and altogether better adapted to its own thoroughly self-interested approach to what the ocean is for.

The call for longer-range thinking is always problematic for a certain mind-set. Or 'the struggle of man against power is the struggle of memory against forgetting', as Milan Kundera, another one of those Czechs I used to read all the time, once put it. Lyme Bay has

witnessed many transformations in our relationship
with the sea. But there is one episode in particular
which should be better known than it is.

—

The Devon Record Office was moved to a business
park on the edge of Exeter at about the same time as
a new Met Office was going up just across the road.
The document I have pre-booked is carried with care
between the reading-room tables. The large cardboard
folder contains particulars relating to five voyages
made to the Arctic between 1754 and 1759. Whales in
any number had by then, evidently, long since disappeared from English waters, but this is a ledger detail-
ing all income and outgoings to and from The Exeter
Whale Fishery Company. At the end of each set of accounts are the signatures of the company's directors,
creatures of habit who met each year in the same coffee house to inspect and sign the columns of figures.
At the end of each voyage there is an entry showing the
payment made to the crew 'when they returned from
Greenland.'

Disbursement Number One: £2150 'for purchase
of a ship in London.' The vessel was re-christened the
Exeter and fitted-out as a whaler on the mudflats at
Lympstone. Harpoons, lances and whale-line, cord-
age and rivets must be purchased. Insurance, coal,
coopers. Sailmakers and smiths present their bills.
The ship would have shared those mud-flats, in the

winter of 1754, with one of the West Country's largest fleets of Newfoundland 'bankers'. Named after the
Grand Banks on which they fished the cod, the bankers travelled west each spring, returning to Lympstone
each autumn.

There were an estimated one hundred of them
plying this route in 1600. These were the fishermen
William Borough and William Gilbert interviewed as
they researched their books about the earth's magnetic
field and there were plenty of them to interview. But
the Whale Fishery Company was not some 'organic'
development of these predecessors. The many Scottish
surnames on the crew-lists are a clue: suitably trained
personnel were unavailable locally. Most whaling companies set up at this time were in the north and east
of England. Exeter's involvement is more complicated
than it first appears.

A quarter of a century had passed before the whales
Davis had noted on his voyages to Greenland began
to be hunted on any systematic basis. The Spitzbergen
whaling grounds were already by then in decline. In
this the Dutch had led the way, so it was Dutch and not
British ports that benefitted. Irked by this, the British
Government tried various schemes to stimulate their
own whaling fleet.

In 1749 they hit upon the crude but effective
method of offering a massive bounty on every tonne
of whale blubber and bone brought back from
Greenland. Exeter might not have the facilities or

experienced crews of its northern competitors, but its cloth trade was in long-term decline and thirty-two of its merchants knew a good deal when they saw one. They subscribed over £5,000 to found the company and less than a year later the shareholders signed their first set of accounts.

The document to which they put their signatures remains to this day a startling window into the day to day operations of such a venture. The ship operated in a punishing environment. After a ship accompanying the *Exeter* became caught in ice in the Davis Straits, money was paid out 'for victuallising 8 men 344 day[s] after the ship was lost @ 6d'. The *Exeter* was in 1757 attacked by a French privateer – England and France were at war over Canada at the time. 'The Coffin and Burying of Ben Courtenay who was killed defending the ship': 19 shillings. Hiring a coach 'to carry the wounded men to Hospital' cost 5 shillings. There are doctor's fees to pay. Thomas Glass is not mentioned but must have heard about it. On the next voyage, £195 are paid out 'for Warlike stores'. There was relief when that expedition returned safely: two shillings and sixpence were paid to 'the messenger who brought News of the Ship's arrival'.

But there was money in 'weighing the whale bone.' There was 'cutting money for 6 fish' at so much a fish. There was money for 'watching the oil while boiling.' And the danger of the work may help explain how well fed the crews were by the standards of the day. '2 Hogsheads of good beef'. Twelve hens supplied the crew with fresh eggs. Mustard seed and cress were grown on board.

At a first glance these accounts are quite unexceptionable. Here is an honourable record of business transactions conducted by scrupulous gentlemen. The destruction of the northern bowhead proceeds but the accounting is exact and the handwriting is immaculate. Candles, tea and coffee. No hint of a scruple. Profits from this company were considerable and will certainly have found their way into the building boom which created some of Exeter's most elegant buildings of this period. The 'whale bone', i.e. baleen, from one journey yields about £800. The oil, about £1100. In those days, you could build some nice houses for that and build them they did. And then more. On 28 March 1758, £1 1s is paid 'To the crew to drink the owner's health.'

It all sounds jolly prosperous. There is nothing here to suggest, say, that any of the directors might be dealing on a private basis, selling company products through intermediaries and profiting royally therefrom. For that information you must turn to the private accounts of the company's treasurer, one Mathew Lee. They are, as luck would have it, preserved in the same archive.

The accounts of our energy companies will read no less strangely to our descendants, as they discover all the updated ways we have found to 'drink the owner's health.' The conferences and the bonuses, sponsorship for the arts. It was, after all, largely for their oil that these creatures were valued. As Rebecca Solnit puts it:

'ultimately the destruction of the Earth is due in part, perhaps in large part, to a failure of the imagination or to its eclipse by systems of accounting that can't count what matters.'

—

The British Government, quite as much in the 21st century as in the 18th, continues to offer excellent illustrations of this. Ben Bradshaw, Minister for Fisheries in 2006 and closely involved with the build-up to the Lyme Bay closure in 2008, is still MP for Exeter. His government's establishment of that original MPA was an act of far-sighted political bravery. Governments since, 'greenest ever' ones included, have rarely matched that courage. Continuing efforts by the dredgers to be readmitted to the MPA and the support they are receiving from some in government should serve to remind us that the 1750s are not as far away as they might seem.

The MPA has, over a decade or so, developed a management structure tailored to its own needs. That the scallop-dredgers have been successfully excluded is down to an alliance of formally trained biologists and responsible fishermen. The fine-scale knowledge of the area, which the fishermen provided, has meshed with that wider-scale, methodical knowledge of marine habitats, which the researchers have brought with them. The fishermen have been fully involved with surveying the sea-bed's recovery.

Marine conservation is popular. Communities around the bay, like the one I live in, are rightly proud that the first of the larger reserves was established here. But the popularity of marine conservation does not always translate into the kind of organised opposition that actually wins. Of those 'protected areas' which have been created around the country, Lyme Bay is among the more fortunate. Others have already seen the readmission of dredgers, as in Cardigan Bay.

In conservation, as in any other field, it is easy enough to say that the best course is to discover the truth and then insist upon it. So, of course, we should. But we can work, also, to deepen the kind of truth we tell. The Devon Wildlife Trust recently launched a campaign to protect the white-beaked dolphins in Lyme Bay. They argue that the white-beaks would benefit from such a measure because they are more sensitive to surface temperature than other species of dolphin. You could protect the cooler areas of the bay and be sure you were protecting them.

They argue also that the nutrient up-welling, abundant in plankton and fish of all kinds which attract the dolphins, is well worth 'future proofing'. Minke whale, basking shark and harbour porpoise have all been recorded, as well as the Balearic shearwater. There are as yet no English Marine Protected Areas for such 'highly mobile marine species', i.e. cetaceans and birds. The white-beaks are clearly resident and therefore well suited to this form of protection.

The Devon Wildlife Trust and the Hadley Centre for Climate Change are based in the same city, yet the campaign has thus far made less than it might have of the climate change implications. It is seeking to protect a marine mammal closely associated with the Arctic, here towards the southern limit of its range. Their continued presence in the bay, in other words, will be directly affected by climate change.

Exeter, as we've seen, is one of the many British cities that enriched themselves through whaling, that is to say, through killing cetaceans for their bone and oil. Whale ships once set out for Greenland through precisely the waters in which the white-beaks are now found. Might this reserve not be some small way to make belated amends? Who, today, shares that indifference to the health of our oceans that is written all over those accounts of the Exeter Whale Fishery Company?

So by all means, in other words, invite TV crews out on boats. Get all the air-time you can. But in the thick of all this awareness-raising, how do we *deepen* that awareness? Or if we are reluctant to do that deepening, then what are we really aiming for? And if the culture of news is not up to this on its own, then we need to supplement it with some other culture that is.

It is often pointed out that a five-year electoral cycle leaves democratically elected politicians trapped in the short-term, unable to respond to or even see something like climate change. Its corollary is less often pointed out: that the telling of longer stories then becomes the responsibility of those who *can* see.

Our attitude towards whaling, for example, has certainly been transformed over the past fifty years but the change goes back further than that. When William Scoresby moved to Torquay in the 1840s he already had an astonishing career behind him. He had first visited the Arctic in 1799, aged ten, on board his father's whaling ship. Father and son alike were much preoccupied by the search for the North-West Passage and together in 1806 had reached latitude 81°12′ N, a record northing at the time.

Scoresby later trained as a scientist and his *Account of the Arctic Regions* (1820) included detailed studies of the bowhead and other cetaceans which were drawn upon by Herman Melville as he wrote *Moby Dick*. Scoresby was the first to argue in a scientific context for the bowhead's great longevity – an insight confirmed by later research. He also studied the earth's magnetism, the structure of snow crystals and water temperature in the Arctic.

Though a native of Yorkshire, it was in a town overlooking Lyme Bay that he chose to end his days, having taken holy orders. There could surely be no more fitting tribute to his life's work – and to the changes in our outlook it helped to bring about – than a dolphin sanctuary in the waters off Torquay.

In campaigns like this one for the white-beaked dolphins, the usual appeal is to science, and rightly so. But this begs an important question. Science may take the measure of things more accurately than any other form of truth. Researchers rightly feel a duty to speak out when they see the life-support systems on which we all depend under threat. The science is quite indispensable but can it *on its own* generate the values which promote acceptance of its authority? Its claim to stand above the fray in which values are contested might seem to disqualify it for this role. Its virtues may but do not always have mass appeal, especially when its message is unwelcome.

That is why scientists who understand the gravity of this know we have to tell a richer, better story. About how the dredgers were excluded from Lyme Bay in 2008 and the sea-bed's recovery since? Certainly. But about Aelfric and his whales and about the 'incredible Number of fish' Daniel Defoe watched being hauled ashore at West Bay, too. About the 'school of mackerel twinkling in the afternoon light', which Thomas Hardy once noticed from Portland Bill. About those whalers drinking 'the owner's health' at Lympstone and the 'bankers' departing each spring for the Newfounde lands and their 'infinite store' of cod. About John Davis setting out from Lyme Bay, with his Paradoxal Compass, in search of a way to China. And about seals deep under the ice, in the waters that still bear his name, collecting data for us as they do so. All of these could and should form part of our case for longer-range thinking and a more deeply considered relationship with the sea.

– Epilogue –

Lyme Bay was always more than just a fishing-ground. When George Somers sailed his *Sea Venture* out of Lyme Regis in 1609, he can have had little idea of what he was setting in motion. His ship was wrecked on Bermuda, then a deserted island, where the crew lived for most of a year before building themselves new boats and completing the journey to America. One of the investors in that voyage was, of course, one William Shakespeare, who read an account of their adventures on the island and knew what to do with it.

Before he directed his film version of *The Tempest*, Derek Jarman wrote the screenplay for a fantastical road movie in which Queen Elizabeth and John Dee drive around the English countryside in an old car. Some of the dialogue from this was re-used in his *Jubilee* (1978) but in the original screenplay there was a scene where the Queen and her Arch-Conjuror rest a while on Chesil Beach. 'My heart rejoiceth in the roar of the surf and the shingle,' the Queen says. 'Yea, a great elixir is the sea-shore,' Dee replies.

And so it is. A place of transformative understanding. People have set out across this bay, reimagining humankind's place in the world as they went. And through efforts like the Marine Protected Area we are doing so again, emulating that 'sea-change' of which Ariel sang. Only last year, Lyme Regis raised its first statue to George Somers. I'm not sure we need to set up new statues, or tear down the old ones, Drake's, Somers', or anyone else's. I would rather that the old ones put us in mind of something new: that a vision of the ocean as, before all else, an opportunity to enrich ourselves has failed. But let us recall, also, that this vision was contested from the start. And even the explorers who shared in that vision – to the extent they did – could not then have known what its consequences would be. It is for us, who do know, to reinterpret this legacy in the light of our knowledge.

Four centuries and more is enough gloating over the *Golden Hinde*'s treasure-laden return. It is time we directed our thoughts to those twenty hours it spent snagged on a reef, about which the official versions are so strikingly reticent. A crew on the brink of panic, further from home than any of them had ever been. A terrible mistake, at one stroke, has thrown the fate and purpose of the entire venture into question. All eyes are on the ship's boat now, as its crew tries and tries to fathom the trouble they are in.

FURTHER READING

Richard Carnac Temple (ed.), *The World Encompassed*, The
    Argonaut Press, 1926 (includes Fletcher's notes with
    other narratives and memoranda of the Famous Voyage

Richard Hakluyt, *The Principal Navigations of the English
    Nation*, 1907 (for Stephen and William Borough and John
    Davis see vols. 1, 2 & 5 respectively)

Philip Hoare, *Leviathan or, The Whale*, Fourth Estate, 2008

Clements R. Markham, *A Life of John Davis*, George Philip
    & Son, 1889

Kit Mayers, *North-East Passage to Muscovy, Stephen Borough
    and the First Tudor Explorations*, Sutton, 2005

Kasper van Ommen (ed.), *The Exotic World of Carolus
    Clusius*, Leiden University Library, 2009

Glyn Parry, *The Arch-Conjuror of England: John Dee*, Yale,
    2013

Jan Patočka, *Essais Hérétiques*, Éditions Verdier, 1999

Stephen Pumphrey, *Latitude and the Magnetic Earth*, Icon
    Books, 2002 (an introduction to William Gilbert)

Callum Roberts *The Unnatural History of the Sea*, Gaia, 2007

Giorgio de Santillana, *The Crime of Galileo*, University of
    Chicago Press, 1956

John Sugden, *Sir Francis Drake*, Pimlico, 2006

D. W. Waters, *The Art of Navigation in Elizabethan and Early
    Stuart Times*, Hollis & Carter, 1958

You can find out more about Portland's Save Our Strip
campaign at https://portsocsfq.wordpress.com.
Read more about the campaign for a Marine Protected Area
for dolphins at www.devonwildlifetrust.org/devon-dolphins.

ACKNOWLEDGEMENTS

Kim Kremer, Charles Wild, Lucy Goodison, John Siddorn, Julian Andrews, Florike Egmond, Peter Mason, Ellie Jones, Tom Brereton, Dave Sales, Carlotta Molfese, Roger Furniss, Philip Hoare, Kit Mayers, Charles Bircham, Peter Jones, Marilyn Northcott, Adam Mars-Jones, Debbie Parnall, Christopher Pidsley, Devon Archives and Local Studies Service, the Dorset and Devon Wildlife Trusts, the Archive of the British Film Institute, The Caird Library, The Bodleian Library, everybody at No. 10 in Bridport.

Other titles from Notting Hill Editions*

A Short History of Power
by Simon Heffer

Taking a panoramic view from the days of Thucydides to the
present, Heffer analyses the motive forces behind the pursuit
of power, and explains in a beautiful argument why history is
destined to repeat itself.

'Heffer's admirably steely tract combines a well-informed
history intelligence with a subtle account of 2,500 years of
Western history.' – *Times Literary Supplement*

The Mystery of Being Human: God, Freedom and the NHS
by Raymond Tallis

In his latest collection of essays, author, physician and humanist
philosopher Raymond Tallis meditates on the complexity of
human consciousness, free will, mathematics, God and eternity.
The philosophical reflections are interrupted by a fierce polemic
'Lord Howe's Wicked Dream', in which Tallis exposes the
'institutionally corrupt' deception intended to destroy the NHS.

Pilgrims of the Air: The Passing of the Passenger Pigeons
by John Wilson Foster

This is the story of the rapid and brutal extinction of the
Passenger Pigeon, once so abundant that they 'blotted out
the sky', until the last bird died on 1st September, 1914. It is
also an evocative story of wild America – the astonishment
that accompanied its discovery, the allure of its natural
'productions', its ruthless exploitation, and a morality tale for
our times.

CLASSIC COLLECTION

The Classic Collection brings together the finest essayists of the past, introduced by contemporary writers.

Drawn from Life – Selected Essays of Michel de Montaigne
Introduced by Tim Parks

Grumbling at Large – Selected Essays of J. B. Priestley
Introduced by Valerie Grove

*Beautiful and Impossible Things
– Selected Essays of Oscar Wilde*
Introduced by Gyles Brandreth

Words of Fire – Selected Essays of Ahad Ha'am
Introduced by Brian Klug

Essays on the Self – Selected Essays of Virginia Woolf
Introduced by Joanna Kavenna

*All That is Worth Remembering
– Selected Essays of William Hazlitt*
Introduced by Duncan Wu